T0247772

Plautus: *Menaechmi*

BLOOMSBURY ANCIENT COMEDY COMPANIONS

Series editors: C. W. Marshall & Niall W. Slater

The Bloomsbury Ancient Comedy Companions present accessible introductions to the surviving comedies from Greece and Rome. Each volume provides an overview of the play's themes and situates it in its historical and literary contexts, recognizing that each play was intended in the first instance for performance. Volumes will be helpful for students and scholars, providing an overview of previous scholarship and offering new interpretations of ancient comedy.

Aristophanes: Frogs, C. W. Marshall
Aristophanes: Peace, Ian C. Storey
Menander: Epitrepontes, Alan H. Sommerstein
Menander: Samia, Matthew Wright
Plautus: Casina, David Christenson
Plautus: Curculio, T. H. M. Gellar-Goad
Terence: Andria, Sander M. Goldberg

Plautus: *Menaechmi*

V. Sophie Klein

BLOOMSBURY ACADEMIC
LONDON • NEW YORK • OXFORD • NEW DELHI • SYDNEY

BLOOMSBURY ACADEMIC
Bloomsbury Publishing Plc
50 Bedford Square, London, WC1B 3DP, UK
1385 Broadway, New York, NY 10018, USA
29 Earlsfort Terrace, Dublin 2, Ireland

BLOOMSBURY, BLOOMSBURY ACADEMIC and the Diana logo are
trademarks of Bloomsbury Publishing Plc

First published in Great Britain 2022

Copyright © V. Sophie Klein, 2022

V. Sophie Klein has asserted her right under the Copyright, Designs and
Patents Act, 1988, to be identified as Author of this work.

Cover design: Terry Woodley
Cover image © Culture Club/Getty Images

All rights reserved. No part of this publication may be reproduced or transmitted in
any form or by any means, electronic or mechanical, including photocopying,
recording, or any information storage or retrieval system, without prior
permission in writing from the publishers.

Bloomsbury Publishing Plc does not have any control over, or responsibility for, any
third-party websites referred to or in this book. All internet addresses given in this
book were correct at the time of going to press. The author and publisher regret
any inconvenience caused if addresses have changed or sites have ceased
to exist, but can accept no responsibility for any such changes.

A catalogue record for this book is available from the British Library.

Library of Congress Cataloging-in-Publication Data
Names: Klein, V. Sophie (Viviane Sophie), author.
Title: Plautus : Menaechmi / by V. Sophie Klein.
Other titles: Bloomsbury ancient comedy companions.
Description: London ; New York : Bloomsbury Academic, 2022. | Series: Bloomsbury
ancient comedy companions | Includes bibliographical references and index.
Identifiers: LCCN 2021026820 (print) | LCCN 2021026821 (ebook) |
ISBN 9781350092723 (paperback) | ISBN 9781350092730 (hardback) |
ISBN 9781350092747 (ebook) | ISBN 9781350092754 (epub)
Subjects: LCSH: Plautus, Titus Maccius. Menaechmi. |
Latin drama (Comedy)–History and criticism.
Classification: LCC PA6568.M43 K54 2022 (print) | LCC PA6568.M43 (ebook) |
DDC 872/.01–dc23
LC record available at https://lccn.loc.gov/2021026820
LC ebook record available at https://lccn.loc.gov/2021026821

ISBN: HB: 978-1-3500-9273-0
       PB: 978-1-3500-9272-3
       ePDF: 978-1-3500-9274-7
       eBook: 978-1-3500-9275-4

Series: Bloomsbury Ancient Comedy Companions

Typeset by RefineCatch Limited, Bungay, Suffolk
Printed and bound in Great Britain

To find out more about our authors and books visit www.bloomsbury.com
and sign up for our newsletters.

To my family,
my favorite cast of characters and
most cherished source of laughter.

Contents

Preface

I am writing this from a rocking chair in my sister's guest-room, which has become my personal writer's retreat every weekend for almost a year now. Beside me, there's an open window letting in a cool spring breeze, a bouquet of tulips, hyacinths, and pussy willows thoughtfully chosen and beautifully arranged by my mum, and a cup of ginger tea made by my brother-in-law at the end of his long workday. My husband has put the kids to bed. It's late now, so the house is unusually quiet. Most of the time it's filled with the irrepressible shouts, laughter, and rumpus of my beloved daughters and nephews, the youngest of which happen to be identical twins. My family takes turns watching them, cooking, and cleaning so that I can write. I spend my breaks playing Pokémon Superhero Space Adventure (i.e. running around and climbing on stuff) in the garden. This is what I hope to remember most from 2020–2021.

First and foremost, I want to thank my family, especially Jon, Arielle, and Emily, for their love and support during this extraordinary time. This book was possible because of you, and it is for you. Next, I'd like to thank my wonderful editors, Toph Marshall and Niall Slater, and Lily Mac Mahon, Alice Wright, Paul King, Merv Honeywood, and the whole team at Bloomsbury, for enriching this book with their expertise, guidance, and encouragement. I'd also like to thank the Boston University Center for the Humanities for generously supporting this project with a Publication Production Award. Special thanks too to Griffin Budde for his incisive and insightful editorial work on the manuscript, as well as to Kyna Hamill, Brian Walsh, Irit Kleiman, Zsuzsa Varheyli, and Sarah Frederick for their invaluable feedback on drafts and their inspiring collegiality. Boundless gratitude to Helen Romero, Holly Benson, Ana Cuna, Megan Byrne, Ismerai 'Izzy' Reyes, Merari 'Mimi' Reyes, Nena Marcelino, Karen Tosh, and Tracey Maclin for brightening our lives each in their own helpful ways. And, finally, my most heartfelt thanks to all of my students over the years and, in particular, my Spring 2021 Roman Comedy class, who successfully proved that *Menaechmi* can still make people laugh, even via a Zoom production during a global pandemic.

TWINtroduction to *Menaechmi*, Plautus and Roman Comedy

Menaechmi: A prologue

Plautus' *Menaechmi* is a rollicking comedy of errors about a pair of long-lost identical twin brothers who reunite after many years and one madcap day of mistaken identity mix-ups. With its fanciful premise, memorable characters and farcical antics, the play is one of the most accessible, influential and enduring examples of Roman Comedy. It's not all bubbly doubling and happy endings, however. While *Menaechmi* showcases a playful plot, sparkling dialogue and dynamic stage action, its humour can also be dark and deeply troubling at times, particularly in its depictions of slavery and misogyny. The playwright balances shtick and social commentary, bumbling tomfoolery and soaring word play to tell a tale that is distinctly Plautine and also part of a much larger comic tradition.

The aim of this book is to provide the essential background information for studying and interpreting the play. It situates *Menaechmi* in its original cultural, theatrical and thematic contexts, and shines a spotlight on the witty language, waggish personalities and wacky shenanigans that shape the story and epitomize Roman Comedy. Chapter 1 sets out an overview of the play, its playwright, and the circumstances of its composition and production (when, where, how, by whom, and for whom *Menaechmi* was originally performed). Chapter 2 investigates *Menaechmi*'s setting, characters and themes. The first section discusses the relationship between the Greek world in which the comedy is set and the Roman world for which it was written. The subsequent sections each focus on a particular 'stock' character, providing the relevant socio-historical background, discussing the characters' representations in this play and in the New Comic tradition, and exploring the themes that arise from their interactions with one another. Chapter 3 looks at the 'bits, banter, and buffoonery' that typify Plautine humour and electrify the script, including metatheatre, word play and physical comedy. It also unpacks the preposterously drawn-out recognition scene. Finally, Chapter 4 presents an overview of Menaechmi's reception, beginning with its first known revival (*c.* 1486) under Ercole I, the Duke of Ferrara, and ending with a survey of notable modern productions. In all, the book explores the timelessness and universality of the play, which is at once a descendant of Greek New Comedy, an emblem of Roman Comedy, and a forebear of English, French, Italian, and broader global drama.

Plot summary

The story takes place in Epidamnus, a Greek city infamous for its hussies and hustlers (258–264). The scene is set on a street in front of two houses: that of Menaechmus and that of his prostitute, Erotium. A prologue, delivered by an unnamed speaker, lays out the back-story (1–76): Once upon a time there was a merchant from Syracuse who had a pair of twin sons named Menaechmus and Sosicles. Leaving Sosicles at home, the merchant took young Menaechmus on a business trip to Tarentum. There, the child was kidnapped by a merchant from Epidamnus who adopted him as his own. Devastated by the loss of his son, the poor father died of grief. Back in Syracuse, the twins' grandfather heard the news and decided to rename the remaining son 'Menaechmus' after his abducted brother and, moreover, himself. To avoid any confusion on the audience's part, the prologue emphatically underscores that *both* twins will be called Menaechmus. Got it? (47–48). Bringing us to the present, he reports that Menaechmus of Epidamnus (E) has grown up, married, and inherited his adopted father's fortune. Menaechmus of Syracuse (S) (originally named Sosicles), meanwhile, has spent many long years searching for his brother and unwittingly arrives this day on his shores.

Following the prologue, we meet Peniculus, the parasite (77–109). A free man, but a slave to his appetite, he sponges food off of others in exchange for flattery. Peniculus has come to call on Menaechmus E, who storms out of his house berating his wife (*matrona*) – still offstage – for her incessant nagging and spying (110–122). With a wink to the audience, Menaechmus E proudly confirms her suspicions: he announces that he is off to dine with his prostitute (123–126) and reveals that he has stolen a cloak (*palla*) from his wife to give to her (127–134). Catching sight of Peniculus, Menaechmus E revels in his roguery, which the parasite praises in exchange for an invitation to the afternoon's festivities. With some more off-colour banter about wives and whores, they make their way over to Erotium's house next door (135–181).

Erotium, the prostitute, greets her lover with professional charm (182–187). Gifting her the pilfered *palla*, Menaechmus E pledges his love for his mistress and his hatred for his wife. He then asks her to prepare a lavish banquet before departing with Peniculus to attend to some business in the forum (188–217). Erotium summons Cylindrus, the cook, to prepare the feast and everyone leaves to go about their affairs (218–225).

Having thus set the stage and established the dynamics between Menaechmus E and four characters in his world – Peniculus, the *matrona*, Erotium and Cylindrus – the playwright finally introduces Menaechmus S at line 226. The travel-weary twin arrives from the harbour with his trusty slave, Messenio. He describes his arduous journey and reaffirms his steadfast commitment to finding his brother (226–246). Messenio is pessimistic, but pledges his support to his master. He warns him, however, to be on his guard in this wicked, decadent, (Epi)damned place (247–272).

At that very moment, Cylindrus returns from the market and initiates the first Mistaken Identity Bit (273–350). Taking him for his twin, the cook greets Menaechmus S and makes casual conversation about the banquet. Menaechmus S, of course, has no idea who Cylindrus is or what he's talking about. Messenio assumes that the cook is trying to scam them. Puzzled by the exchange, Cylindrus tries to jog his memory, calling Menaechmus by his name and recalling his parasite, his prostitute, and even his house, pointing-distance from where they stand. Confusion ensues, seemingly confirming Messenio's presumptions about Epidamnus and the scoundrels that live there.

Menaechmus S and Messenio scarcely have time to process the encounter with Cylindrus before Erotium enters and sets the second Mistaken Identity Bit in motion (351–445). She calls to Menaechmus S and attempts to seduce him indoors. The young man is baffled by this turn of events while Messenio dismisses it once more as a con. Erotium tries to set things straight by recounting the events of the morning in vivid detail – parasite, *palla* and all – and even correctly identifies Menaechmus S's native land and lineage. She then hands him the wife's cloak and asks him to have it altered. Confused but intrigued, Menaechmus S decides to play along. He goes indoors with Erotium, sending a disapproving Messenio away.

Next, Peniculus returns from the forum grumbling because he has lost track of Menaechmus E and, by extension, his free lunch (446–465). At that moment, he catches sight of Menaechmus S, wearing a garland and carrying the wife's cloak, leaving Erotium's house. The parasite deduces that his patron deliberately ditched him in order to dine alone with Erotium, prompting the third Mistaken Identity Bit (466–523). Menaechmus S, meanwhile, rejoices at his unexpected good fortune: not only has he enjoyed Erotium's hospitality, but he has also made off with an expensive cloak! Fuming, Peniculus confronts Menaechmus S about his betrayal, which the young man naturally denies. They trade insults and Peniculus storms off, vowing that his patron will be sorry.

With his head still spinning, Menaechmus S is approached by yet another character from this strange new world: it is Erotium's maid (*ancilla*), delivering a bracelet that Menaechmus E had also stolen from his wife. In a fourth Mistaken Identity Bit (524–558), the maid conveys Erotium's request that he take it to the jeweller. Menaechmus S greedily accepts the bracelet and, laden with riches, he leaves to find Messenio and get out of town before his luck turns.

Tension mounting, the unnamed wife of Menaechmus E finally bursts onto the scene at line 559 with Peniculus in tow. She is furious with her husband for stealing from her and giving her things to his mistress. Wife and parasite position themselves just out of sight and prepare to ambush Menaechmus E, who presently returns from the forum (559–570). They eavesdrop as he mopes about the demands of the patron-client relationship and sulks about having squandered his day of play with Erotium, for whom he stole the cloak (571–601). Having heard his full confession, the wife steps out and lays into Menaechmus E for his infidelity and larceny. Peniculus piles on with complaints about his lost lunch, insisting that he saw Menaechmus E leaving Erotium's house only moments ago. In a fifth Mistaken Identity Bit (602–664), Menaechmus E truthfully disavows that most recent encounter, while falsely denying all other accusations. When the plaintiffs persist, he finally gives in and promises to get the cloak back. The wife locks him out of the house until he does. Having fallen out of favour with patron and wife, the parasite stalks off to the forum to find a new meal ticket (665–667).

Left alone onstage, Menaechmus E cheekily boasts that he's just as happy to be sent next door. Walking headlong into the sixth Mistaken Identity Bit (668–700), he greets Erotium and asks her to return the cloak. Growing increasingly annoyed with this nonsense, the prostitute asserts that she already gave him the *palla* along with a bracelet. Menaechmus E, of course, denies having seen her since he left for the forum that morning. Erotium thinks he's trying to cheat her and sends him away. Confused and kicked out of both houses, Menaechmus E wanders offstage to make sense of his situation.

As one brother exits, the other enters looking for Messenio and carrying the focal cloak. The wife reappears and catches sight of him. In the seventh Mistaken Identity Bit (701–752), the wife and Menaechmus S trade scathing barbs. After a lively and extended volley of insults, the *matrona* announces that her father will settle the argument. Right on cue, the old man (*senex*) enters, his slow gait in sharp contrast to the suddenness of his appearance (753–774). The wife appeals to her father, reviling her husband's misconduct. Surprisingly, the *senex* takes his son-in-law's side: he tells his daughter that she is supposed to please her husband, not spy on him, and he even supports Menaechmus E's decision to cheat on her with the prostitute next door (775–808). It is only when the wife reports that Menaechmus E is stealing from her that the old man is willing to reconsider his stance.

In an eighth Mistaken Identity Bit (809–875), the *senex* interrogates Menaechmus S, who is utterly perplexed by these people and their problems. Since the wife and her father assume that he has lost his mind, Menaechmus S decides to play along. In a moment rife with comic potential, he pretends to be a madman, raving so frantically that he sends the *matrona* running home in terror and the *senex* hobbling off in search of a doctor. Left alone onstage, Menaechmus S again concludes that the time has come to hightail it out of there (876–881).

Almost immediately, the old man returns with a doctor (*medicus*) in tow (882–898). In a ninth Mistaken Identity Bit (899–965), they come upon an unsuspecting Menaechmus E, who reflects upon the bizarre events of the day. In a foul mood, he has no patience for the old man or the doctor who confront him cautiously. His anger seems to confirm their diagnosis of madness. They go off to arrange for his capture and delivery to the doctor's house for observation, leaving Menaechmus E alone onstage to contemplate his sanity.

At this point, Messenio dutifully returns having followed his master's orders: he has taken care of their belongings and arrived at the appointed time and place to escort Menaechmus S safely away from this wicked wonderland (966–989). Suddenly the *senex* reappears with reinforcements who pounce on Menaechmus E and attempt to subdue him. In a tenth Mistaken Identity Bit (990–1049), Messenio leaps to his 'master's' rescue, declaring his loyalty and valiantly fighting off his attackers. Menaechmus E thanks this stranger for his help; Messenio asks for his freedom in return. Menaechmus E honestly asserts that Messenio is no slave of his, accidentally freeing him. Delighted by this turn of events, Messenio rejoices at his newfound freedom and requests to continue living with his former master as his client. An elated Messenio runs off to collect their things, leaving Menaechmus E confused, but amused at his topsy-turvy day. He pops into Erotium's house to try to plead his case and win back both mistress and cloak.

A split second later, Messenio and Menaechmus S re-enter, engaged in Mistaken Identity Bit number eleven (1050–1059): Messenio explains that he just rescued his master from a fight and won his freedom, while Menaechmus S denies that either ever happened. Meanwhile, Menaechmus E steps out of Erotium's house, bewildered by the whole cloak and bracelet business. In this twelfth and final Mistaken Identity Bit (1060–1162), the twins finally meet face to face. While the brothers take an absurdly long time to grasp the situation, Messenio quickly catches on and offers to solve the mystery in exchange for his freedom, for real this time. He guides their conversation to its natural conclusion, whereupon the brothers recognize one another and forgive and forget all the transgressions of the dreamlike day. Menaechmus S invites his brother to return to their native land with him. Menaechmus E agrees and plans to auction off all his Epidamnian possessions, including his wife, at the earliest opportunity. But first, the brothers celebrate and the play arrives at its happy ending.

Plautus: Life and work

Plautus (*c.* 254–184 BCE) is one of the most important and influential playwrights in the Western comic tradition. Extremely popular and prolific in his lifetime, his work continued to be performed for centuries after his death. It inspired a pantheon of artists including Shakespeare, Molière and Sondheim, as well as a variety of genres ranging from *commedia dell'arte* to modern television sitcoms.

Plautus' comedies represent the earliest extant Latin literature. We have fragments of earlier and contemporary authors, but only Plautus' work survives generally complete from this early period.[1] His popularity is evident in the sheer number of plays attributed to him during and immediately after his lifetime; by the late second / early first century BCE, there were approximately 130 'Plautine' comedies in circulation. These scripts were likely working copies of the plays emended by actors and producers. The literary historian Varro (116–27 BCE) established the official Plautine corpus of twenty-one plays – twenty of which survive mostly intact, plus *Vidularia* which exists only as a fragment – by reviewing the existing lists of his comedies and identifying the ones that appeared most consistently.[2] These have been passed down to us via centuries of hand copying until the invention of the printing press in the fifteenth century.[3] They enjoyed a surge of revived interest during the Renaissance and have been continually studied, adapted and performed ever since.

Despite Plautus' fame and success, we know essentially nothing about his life.[4] One prevailing, but suspect, narrative purports that he was born in Sarsina, Umbria and that he started out working behind the scenes in the theatre before losing all his money in a business venture and being forced to work in a mill to repay his debts. While toiling away in the mill, he managed to dash off a few plays, the success of which enabled him to pay off his debts and become a full-time author. While this is an attractive origin-story, Plautus was probably either a slave or a free man of low social status, like most ancient theatre-folk, who made a name for himself through his art.

Even his name, however, is dubious. 'Titus Maccius Plautus' is a little too on the nose for a comedian: 'Titus' may have been slang for 'Phallus' or 'Dick', 'Maccius' means 'Son of a Clown' and recalls the name of a stock character from Atellan farce, and 'Plautus' means 'Flat(foot)', a colloquial term for a Roman mime performer. As Gratwick (1993: 3) remarks, 'While both Maccius and Plautus are real Roman names, it is clearly incredible that a boy named T. Maccius Plautus 'Dickie Clownson Tumbler' just happened to grow up to be a successful and prolific comic dramatist.' More likely, the playwright adopted a stage name.

Similarly elusive are his dates. While we can identify the general time period that Plautus was writing in (late third / early second century BCE), we have frustratingly little evidence to help us pinpoint exactly when his work was composed or performed. Only two production notices (*didascaliae*) survive, prefacing the scripts for *Stichus* and *Pseudolus*. These include the names of the magistrates at the time, enabling us to date these plays to 200 BCE and 191 BCE, respectively, though even these records are questionable.[5] Two fleeting textual allusions, one to a military campaign that must have preceded the end of the Second Punic War in 201 BCE (*Cistellaria* 201–2) and the other to an incident involving the playwright Naevius in 205 BCE (*Miles Gloriosus* 211–12), are all the concrete 'facts' that we have to work with. The rest is conjecture. While sometime in 190s BCE is possible, there is no conclusive evidence for the date of *Menaechmi*.[6]

Still, Plautus' work is a distinct product of its time. The third century BCE was a transformative era in Roman history, characterized by vast military expansion and dynamic cultural revolution. The Romans were constantly at war during this early period, both at home and abroad. Having conquered the Italian peninsula, they were eager to expand their growing empire. Their main rivals for control of the Western Mediterranean were the Carthaginians, Phoenician colonists with powerful military and commercial resources, based in modern-day Tunisia. They fought three major wars against one another, with Rome victorious in each one. Plautus grew up in the aftermath of the First Punic War (261–241 BCE) and saw the Romans defeat the Carthaginians in the Second Punic War (218–201 BCE), but he would not have lived to see their final victory and the destruction of Carthage at the conclusion of the Third Punic War (149–146 BCE).

During these long and bloody years, Rome was continually fighting on several fronts with enemies from all over the Mediterranean world. As Richlin (2005: 17) poignantly notes, 'each war made new roles for people: soldier, veteran, prisoner of war, refugee, exile, slave, widow, orphan, prostitute'. These are the characters that populate Plautus' stage. They were also the spectators that populated his audience. Theatregoers who had personal experience with the tragic realities of kidnapped children, prostitution, or slavery likely had complicated reactions to these 'comic' features of *Menaechmi*.[7]

Additionally, the wars brought the Romans into widespread contact with new people and new customs as never before. Early battles with Greek kings and city-states in Sicily and Southern Italy, in particular, as well as later ones with the Macedonians in Northern Greece, introduced the Romans to the art and ethos of the Greek world. Rome fell under Greece's spell, and it avidly absorbed everything from its drama and philosophy to its gods.

The wars, then, set the stage for a cultural sea change of seismic proportions. They brought an influx of wealth as well as foreign people and perspectives into Rome, creating a crucible for forging a blended, but distinct, national identity. Greek culture played a defining role in this metamorphosis, despite backlash from conservatives, such as Cato the Elder (239–149 BCE), who denounced it as a threat to traditional Roman morals and sensibilities. Over time, however, Rome developed a clear literary voice that both stood apart from and also harmonized with its Greek models.

Greek new comic and Italian dramatic origins

Roman Comedy did not develop in a vacuum. It evolved over centuries and across cultures out of many and diverse theatrical forms. Chief among these were: Greek drama, Atellan farce, and mime.

Greek drama is by far the most conspicuous influence on Plautus. His plays are almost always set in the Greek world, his characters often have Greek names, and, unless plot points demand otherwise, they wear Greek costumes. Indeed, the genre of Roman Comedy comes to be called the *fabula palliata* or 'plays in Greek clothing' (after the Latin word for a Greek cloak, *pallium*). Even more to the point, Plautus frequently identifies his closest Greek models – including Philemon, Diphilus and Menander – directly by name, often in prologues where he explicitly identifies the Greek play that he is adapting (Cf. *Asinaria* 10–11, *Mercator* 9–10, *Trinummus* 18–19 and *Vidularia* 6–7).

In fact, Plautus' debt to the Greeks extends further back than these 'New Comic' poets of the late fourth to mid-third centuries BCE. Elements of his form and style can be traced all the way to the fifth century BCE and found in both comedy and tragedy. As Gratwick (1993: 8) notes, for example, the 'themes of misapprehension, deception, separation, and recognition' that are so central to *Menaechmi* are also hallmarks of Euripidean drama.

Plautus also seems to have been influenced by Epicharmus, an early fifth-century Greek comic writer and philosopher who lived in Sicily. Only fragments of his work survive, but pieced together they suggest that he wrote social comedies and character studies, in addition to mythological travesties. One sizeable fragment from his *Hope or Wealth* is particularly germane to our study of *Menaechmi*:

> Dining with whoever's willing – all he needs to do is issue an invitation! – as well as with whoever's unwilling – and then there's no need for an invitation. When I'm there, I'm on my best behavior, and I generate a lot of laughs and flatter the man who's hosting the party; if someone wants to quarrel with him, I attack the guy and get similar grief back. Then, after I've eaten and drunk a lot, I leave.
>
> Athenaeus, VI, 235f-236a[8]

Here, Epicharmus paints one of the earliest dramatic portrait of the parasite, a figure that Plautus develops with Peniculus in *Menaechmi*, Artotrogus in *Miles Gloriosus*, and Gelasimus in *Stichus*.[9] Praised by Plato (*Theatetus* 152e) as the 'best of comic poets' and recognized by Aristotle (*Poetics* 1448a) as one of the originators of comedy, Epicharmus seems to have left an indelible mark on the comic tradition. Indeed, Horace (*Epistles* 2.1.58) names him as one of Plautus' key models. The dearth of surviving evidence, however, prevents us from fully understanding the scope of his influence.

Plautus also drew inspiration from Athenian Comedy. The nature of the genre changed so radically between the fifth and third centuries BCE that scholars have found it useful to categorize it in three stages: 'Old' (486–404 BCE), 'Middle' (404–336 BCE) and 'New' (336-c. 250 BCE). By observing the transformation of Greek Comedy over this period, we can better understand how Roman Comedy developed out of it in turn.

Greek 'Old Comedy', preserved in the work of Aristophanes (*c*. 450– *c*. 388), often depicted fantastical tales or political satires. They were spectacular musical extravaganzas, featuring outlandishly festooned singing and dancing choruses, with language as bawdy as it was lyrical. Inextricably tied to its time and place, a key aspect of its humour relied on the audience's knowledge of the fifth-century Athenian politics and personalities that it regularly referenced. This lively style of comedy flourished for almost a century. With the defeat of Athens at the end of the Peloponnesian War in 404 BCE, ensuing political, social and economic austerity subdued its splashy style. Audiences seem to have become more interested in small, personal stories about everyday family life than grand, public ones with strong civic messages.

Greek 'Middle Comedy' survives only in brief quotations. A transitional category, it seems to bridge the gap between Old and New by concentrating more predominantly on social types and themes, as well as mythological travesty.[10] Surviving titles like 'The Miser', 'The Misanthrope', and – most tantalizing with respect to *Menaechmi* – 'The Twins', pose intriguing questions about their content and the breadth of their influence. Duckworth (1952: 23) observes that 'while no plot can be restored, . . . a few broad generalizations are nevertheless possible ... Plays on mythological themes were popular, but more and more the action dealt with everyday life and often centred about a love story and its complications. As to characters, in addition to family types (husbands, wives, sons, slaves) the parasite, the soldier, the courtesan appeared more frequently.'

By the time 'New Comedy' comes into its own, the stories fully revolve around the domestic lives of familiar character types.[11] They follow the same basic formula in which a family member, a lover, a source of wealth, and / or freedom is literally or figuratively lost and often, but not always, found. Misunderstandings ensue leading to comic commotion and confusion before a clever plan or a convenient twist of fate delivers a socially normative resolution. At once personal and also universal, they are stories about love and authority in the home.

These New Comic plays bear little resemblance to those of Old Comedy that they succeed. The dialogue, in verse, continues to be sung as well as spoken, though the language relaxes somewhat over time to sound more colloquial. Gone are the larger than life, cartoonish caricatures of Aristophanes. In their place is a recurring cast of everyday figures, strikingly more naturalistic in language, manner and costume. The chorus' function is greatly diminished as well. From playing a leading role in the storytelling and spectacle, it effectively becomes a 'living curtain', marking act divisions with brief musical interludes. Furthermore, the jokes in New Comedy rely much less on localized references, making it more adaptable for playwrights and more accessible to broader audiences.

This is the style of Greek Comedy that most directly influenced Plautus and his contemporaries. The names of sixty-four New Comic writers survive, including Diphilus, Philemon and Menander. Of these, Menander (341–290 BCE) stands apart as the most frequently quoted, extensively praised, and widely respected comic writer in antiquity. Plutarch and Quintilian celebrate his polished style, his gift of invention, and his versatility with respect to characters, situations and emotions. Above all, the ancient critics marvel at his meticulous mimesis of life (Plutarch, *Moralia* 10.59; Quintilian IO 10.1.69.). Aristophanes of Byzantium famously mused: 'O Menander and Life, which of you imitated the other?' (Syrianus, *Commentary on Hermogenes* 22.24–23.11).

His long-lost work was recovered relatively recently with the discovery of several substantial papyrus fragments and one more or less complete play, *Old Cantankerous* (*Dyskolos*), in the twentieth century. The 1968 publication of a sizeable fragment of *The Double Deceiver* (*Dis Exapatôn*) led to one of the most exciting breakthroughs in the study of ancient comedy. Recognizing it as the model for Plautus' *The Bacchis Sisters* (*Bacchides*), scholars were able to study a Plautine Comedy side by side with its Greek source for the first time and evaluate the extent to which Plautus faithfully adhered to and artfully departed from his model.[12] They discovered that, while he occasionally translated

Menander's script word for word, he also took significant creative liberties with it: Plautus amplified the comic tone by introducing additional word play, metrical variety and musical accompaniment; he reimagined Menander's nuanced, life-like characters in bolder, more one-dimensional forms; and he fine-tuned the flow of the original script by adding or deleting speeches and patching up the breaks that divided Menander's work into five-acts.[13] Similar activity can also be detected throughout *Menaechmi*.

Though a subject of some scholarly dispute, there now seems to be a general consensus that *Menaechmi* was based, at least in part, on a Greek original.[14] Neither the play nor the playwright are named by Plautus,[15] but salient features like its twin-driven mistaken identity premise, its distinctive character types, and even the kinds of jokes that these characters tell, strongly suggest a close kinship with Greek New Comedy.[16]

The most compelling evidence of a Greek original is the structure of *Menaechmi*, which neatly maps onto the five-act format of Menander's plays. Though Plautus did away with the formal act-breaks, like all Roman comedians seem to have done, he nevertheless retained the basic movements of the Greek original here, while adjusting them, often to comic effect. Legrand (1910: 475–76) hypothesizes that the original act-breaks correspond to lines 225, 445, 700, and 881 in the Roman Comedy,[17] evenly dividing the play between the twins: Menaechmus E is the protagonist of Acts 1 and 5 (except for the denouement), and Menaechmus S is the protagonist of Acts 2 and 4.[18] The brothers share Act 3 and, of course, the final recognition scene. The term 'clockwork' is often used in the scholarship to describe the mechanical sequencing of the action. The structure, then, offers an apt sense of symmetry to a play about doubles. It also helps the audience keep the identities of each twin straight, while the characters muddle through their confusion onstage.

In smoothing over the original act divisions, Plautus accelerated the comic pace of *Menaechmi* and created new opportunities for metatheatrical humour. One of the most effective illustrations of this is the return of the *senex* at line 881, who, after initially lamenting the slow-pace and feebleness of his age, is able to leave, track down the doctor, and return onstage with him within the span of five lines. Without the act-break to account for the passage of time, the old man's supersonic turnaround becomes a bonus joke in Plautus' comedy.

Scholars have identified numerous other examples of Plautine innovation to *Menaechmi*'s original. Lowe (2019: 221), among others, has posited that Plautus likely introduced additional musical content (five polymetric *cantica*), and either invented or expanded whole scenes such as the one with Erotium's maid and the bracelet (524–558), the madness episode of Menaechmus S (829/830–875), the doctor's examination of Menaechmus E (889–965), and the ludicrously long recognition scene (1060–1162).[19] Using Greek New Comedy as both an archetype and a springboard, then, Plautus perpetuated the comic tradition and also made it his own.

In addition to Greek drama, native Italian theatre played an important role in the development of Roman Comedy.[20] This comprised a wide range of performative genres, including music, dance, acrobatics, burlesque, invective and improvised skits, among others. Because they were unscripted in Plautus' time, our limited and unreliable evidence amounts to comments of later critics and fragments of later scripted forms. These provide only glimpses of the characters, scenarios and devices that were massively popular in Plautus' time and remained so for centuries afterward. Let us focus on two forms, in particular, whose imprint can be seen on *Menaechmi*: Atellan farce and mime.

Atellan farce *(Fabulae Atellanae)* is named after the Oscan town of Atella in Campania, Southern Italy, where the genre is thought to have originated.[21] Like Roman Comedy – and indeed Greek New Comedy – it also featured a recurring cast of stock characters, instantly recognizable by the conventional masks they wore: Pappus ('Grandpappy'), Maccus ('Clown'), Bucco ('Fool'), Dossennus ('Hunchback') and Manducus ('Glutton'), among others. The surviving titles suggest that the stories regularly reshuffled and recast these figures in a variety of comic roles: *Pappus the Farmer, Maccus the Maiden,*

Maccus the Soldier, and – notably with respect to *Menaechmi* – *The Maccus Twins* and *The Two Dossennuses.*[22]

In Plautus' time, *Atellanae* were improvised by troupes of experienced actors who could work in carefully honed routines full of lively slapstick and witty banter as they saw fit. Plautus seems to have run with this technique, allowing ample space for physical comedy, word play and ad-libbing in his work. In our play, this is perhaps best illustrated by the scene in which Menaechmus S feigns a fit of madness and frightens away his brother's wife and father-in-law.[23] The scene provides an ideal opportunity for skilled actors to exploit dynamic movement, verbal fireworks and the freedom to expand the bit if it was working well or contract it as needed. As Gratwick (1993: 15) notes,

> [Plautus is determined] to create in his audience the impression that there *is* no script and that they are watching a 'happening' – not so much a slice of life surreptitiously spied on, but an improvised performance by Italian actors masquerading in Greek costume. The play is, literally, a game in which we spectators know that the players know that we know what they are up to; an elaborate game of deception.

Mime was another form of unscripted, comic entertainment that was popular in and around Rome in Plautus' time.[24] The precise meaning of the term remains a mystery since it was used broadly and inconsistently to describe a wide range of theatrical forms in antiquity and has no obvious connection to what we might call 'mime' today. Fantham (1989: 154) attempts to define it as follows: 'whatever did not fit the generic categories of tragedy or comedy, Atellan or the Italian togate comedy, was mime: a narrative entertainment in the *media* of speech, song and dance'. Its two distinguishing features were that: (1) its performers were unmasked and (2) the troupe could include women. Terracotta figurines of mime actors support these facts, along with the tradition that players performed barefoot, hence the nickname 'Flat-Foots'.

Adultery seems to have been a dominant theme of mime.[25] Stories about cheating lovers were wildly popular with audiences spanning the social spectrum. They also contributed to the genre's notorious and vulgar reputation, the target of much conservative criticism. Unabashedly erotic in nature, mimes could feature costumes that simulated nudity by means of anatomically exaggerated bodysuits, tights and dangling phalli. According to later sources, female actresses could even appear in the nude.[26]

While less graphic in its depiction of adultery, the affair between Menaechmus E and Erotium carries on this comic tradition. The audience listens in as Menaechmus E boasts about his extramarital exploits, woos Erotium, gets caught, and then suffers the consequences, namely the wrath of both his mistress and his wife. The dramatic tension literally doubles when Menaechmus S enters the picture and unwittingly complicates matters for his brother. While the overarching plot of the play centres on the recognition and reunion of the titular twins, much of the action along the way is in fact driven by the adultery theme and the comic conflicts that it generates. In that regard, Roman Comedy and mime tap into a shared comedic formula.

Greek drama, Atellan farce and mime represent only a handful of the sources that inspired Plautus and his fellow Roman comedians. Other more elusive dramatic forms, such as Fescinnine Verses – an early form of improvisational invective – and *phylax* dramas – farcical burlesques preserved primarily on fourth-century BCE vase paintings from Southern Italy – contributed to the rich, multi-layered character of Roman Comedy in ways we may never fully appreciate. As Segal (2001: xxi) notes, 'like Shakespeare and Molière, Plautus begs, borrows and steals from every conceivable source – including himself. But once the play begins, all literary debts are cancelled and everything is 100 per cent Plautus.'

Cultural context of performance: *Ludi*; actors; audience

When, where, by whom, and for whom was *Menaechmi* originally performed? Like all Roman comedies, *Menaechmi* would have been presented at a Roman public festival. These festivals (*ludi*) were important sacred and social occasions, bringing all levels of the Roman hierarchy together to participate in shared worship and entertainment. The programme combined religious rituals, such as processions, sacrifices and feasts in honour of a god, with dazzling spectacles like theatrical performances, chariot races, boxing matches and gladiatorial combat. The Romans held four main state-sponsored festivals over the course of the year – the *Ludi Megalenses* (April), *Ludi Apollinares* (July), *Ludi Romani* (September) and *Ludi Plebii* (November) – along with lesser *ludi*, such as private ones held for funerals. The main *ludi* were financed by the Senate and subsidized by aediles, low-level magistrates in charge of organizing and overseeing festival events. An ambitious aedile might draw from his personal wealth to embellish the event and drum up popular support as he worked his way up the political ladder (*cursus honorum*).

In the days leading up the *ludi*, temporary wooden theatres were constructed for the performances. Plautus makes a metatheatrical joke about them at *Menaechmi* 402–404, when Menaechmus S compares his ship to a wooden theatre. Goldberg (1998) has elegantly argued that the locations of the theatres likely aligned with the religious context of the *ludi* as well as the existing architecture of the city. He posits, for example, that the temple of the Magna Mater on the western slope of the Palatine Hill would have been a logical performance venue for the *Ludi Megalenses,* which were held in that goddess's honour. A stage could be erected in front of the temple with its steps serving as seating for as many as 2,000 audience members. The temple of Apollo at the north end of the Forum Boarium would have been similarly appropriate for the *Ludi Apollinares.* Various locations around the Roman Forum – including the Comitium, Temple of Castor and Pollux, and Temple of Saturn – likely served as performance spaces during the *Ludi Romani* and some lesser *ludi.* Moore (1998: 137), among others, has noted that the famous speech of the *choragus* at Plautus' *Curculio* 462 calls the audience's attention to several specific locations in and around the forum. He observes that 'almost everything on the tour would be visible to the *choragus* and his audience, and spectators would actually be watching the play from some of the locations cited'.

The first permanent stone theatre in Rome, the Theatre of Pompey, was not built until 55 BCE; the makeshift theatres of Plautus' time would have been much more modest in scale. Evidence from fourth-century BCE Southern Italian red-figure vases, later wall paintings, and the plays themselves suggest that a stage generally comprised a simple elevated platform (*proscaenium*), likely accessible by a low ramp or staircase on all sides, and a wooden backdrop (*scaena*) depicting a generic street in front of two or three houses. The audience would have sat on temporary wooden benches or existing urban structures. The sights, sounds and smells of the city would have permeated the performance space, adding atmospheric colour and context to the theatre-going experience.

As in Shakespeare's time, Plautus' actors were likely all men. Female roles would have been performed in drag, to indeterminate degrees of realism. The average actor was probably either a slave or a free man of low social status.[27] As such, his offstage role would have added complex metatheatrical dimensions to his onstage one(s). Jokes about slave torture, a recurring feature of Roman Comedy (e.g. Messenio's *canticum* at 966–989), would have been charged with poignant layers of meaning, depending on whether the actor delivering them was himself either a slave or a free man.

The average actor, then, embodied paradox: a man who could play a woman, a slave who could play a free person, a slave who could play a slave who was the hero of the story. Additionally, as Richlin (2005: 21) has observed, he was likely a non-native Latin-speaker, delivering his lines in Latin, pretending to be a 'native Roman' with a Greek name in a story set in 'Greece'. In the religiously, socially, temporally circumscribed setting of Roman Comedy, an actor had unique freedom to cross boundaries that normally defined Rome's rigid hierarchy.

Plautus' audience was diverse and dynamic. It comprised individuals from all levels of society: men, women and children, high- and low-status, local and foreign, people whose lives had been touched either directly or indirectly by war. The plays themselves offer the most compelling evidence of the audience's composition. The prologue of 'The Little Carthaginian' (*Poenulus*), for example, famously invokes prostitutes, lictors, slaves, free men, nurses with children, matrons and their husbands, confirming their attendance at the performance. Actors regularly broke down the 'fourth wall' (an anachronistic term, derived from naturalistic theatre) through direct address or metatheatrical nods to their audience, creating an intimate, reciprocal relationship with them.[28] When Menaechmus E first enters, for example, he confides in the audience, lobbying for our empathy as he complains about his wife's intolerable shrewishness. In so doing, he cultivates a sense of comic camaraderie and sets the tone for the play.

Practicalities of performance

a) Music and dance

Like all of Plautus' plays, *Menaechmi* was a musical. Though not a single melody survives from this or any other Roman Comedy, textual clues, especially meter, can help us imagine the prominent role that music must have played in a performance.[29] For the most part, dialogue written in *iambic senarii*, like the prologue (1–76), was spoken and unaccompanied, while passages composed in other meters, like the first scene (77–225), were sung and accompanied by a flute-player (*tibicen*). The libretto alternated between spoken verses (*diverbium*) and sung passages (*cantica* and recitatives) to create exciting and expressive rhythmic and musical variations. It also established a sense of structure by signalling units of action in the plot.

   Menaechmi is especially noteworthy for the ways in which it uses music to create contrast between characters, notably the titular twins.[30] As Moore (1999: 138) observes, Menaechmus E is always accompanied by music and, in fact, he introduces musical accompaniment into previously unaccompanied scenes at each of his entrances except the last (1060). By contrast, whenever Menaechmus S enters a scene, he brings the music to a halt, with the exception of his last entrance (1050), and his speech remains unaccompanied until he 'is affected by a music-bringing character from Epidamnus: Erotium after his first entrance, the old man after his third'. Music, or the lack thereof, then, underscores the identity of each twin and helps the audience keep their Menaechmi straight.

Moore (1999) offers an elegant interpretation of this pattern: He posits that Plautus uses music to draw a dichotomy between the brothers' seriousness. Menaechmus E embodies the 'pleasure principle' or comic fun at the heart of the play, whether he is parading his wife's *palla* or boasting of his plans with Erotium.[31] Menaechmus S, on the other hand, is the straight-man on a solemn mission to find his long-lost brother. Music emphasizes the former's emotion, while unaccompanied speech reinforces the latter's self-control. It encourages the audience to root for the more playful character in the Saturnalian spirit of comedy.

In addition to playing a key role in characterization, music also contributes to emotional tone and stage action. The 'mad scene' (829/830–875), offers a compelling example of this. The musical accompaniment begins with the entrance of the old man (753), continues throughout Menaechmus S's feint of madness, and ceases when he drops the act. It provides an aptly energetic soundtrack to all the commotion. Likewise, when the old man sends his slaves to forcefully capture Menaechmus and bring him to the doctor (990–1020), the ensuing fight between Messenio, Menaechmus E and the slaves plays out in a lively recitative and *iambic canticum*, complementing the frenetic choreography that must have accompanied this scene.

Having established a musical vocabulary for the play, then, Plautus employs it one last time to herald the happy ending. Changing the pattern, the accompaniment no longer stops when Menaechmus S re-enters for the final time (1050). This striking variation signals to the audience that the serious brother has at last adapted to the comic world of the play, anticipating the reunion of the brothers and the harmonious resolution of the plot.

b) Masks

Masks were a regular feature of ancient Greek and Roman drama, and they would have been especially useful here in *Menaechmi*.[32] Their

primary function was to classify character types according to age and
sex: young man, old man, male slave, young woman, old woman. Wigs
and beards complemented the masks, with white hair signifying old age
and dark hair signifying youth. Three redheaded slaves are also
described in the extant plays: Leonida (*Asin.* 400), Pseudolus (*Pseud.*
1218), and Phormio (*Phorm.* 51). Masks made it as easy as possible for
the audience to immediately identify the *dramatis personae* and project
a basic set of expectations onto them, informed by other plays in which
the masks appeared. The playwright could then develop or depart from
these expectations as he saw fit.

Masks would have played a particularly important role in *Menaechmi*.
In addition to marking Messenio as a slave and the father-in-law as an
old man, they would have reinforced the resemblance of the titular
twins throughout the play, rendering them truly identical. In fact, only
one mask is necessary for an actor to play both brothers until they come
face to face with one another in the final scene.

Masks also facilitated an actor's ability to play multiple roles. Greek
dramatists, from the fifth-century Athenian tragedians to the third-
century New Comedians, regularly composed their plays so that three
performers could share all the speaking roles. This so-called 'Rule of
Three Actors' could add meaningful metatheatrical layers to a
performance, as the playwright exploited the audience's awareness of
the doubling to draw connections between characters played by the
same actor.[33]

Roman playwrights, however, largely abandoned this convention.
Four or five speaking characters regularly appear onstage with one
another in Roman Comedy. It is especially striking, then, that *Menaechmi*
does in fact allow for the 'Rule of Three Actors'. It is entirely possible to
stage *Menaechmi* with only three speaking performers and indeed with
the same actor playing both twins right up until the finale.[34] Scholars
often identify this as a remnant of the Roman play's Greek original.

The script features a total of eleven speaking roles, plus an
indeterminate number of mute extras.[35] While it would have been
possible to cast a single actor in each role, a variety of factors, ranging

from metatheatrical value (the effect of having the same actor play multiple roles) to economy (the need to pay each player!), likely limited the size of the troupe.

Damen (1989: 413–14) has proposed a convincing division of roles that optimizes the metatheatrical potential of the doubling and enhances the impact of the extended recognition scene. In his schema, Actor 1 plays both Menaechmi lending risible realism to their resemblance throughout the play. Actor 2 plays Peniculus and Messenio, drawing satiric connections between the related roles of parasite and slave. Actor 3 plays both Erotium and the wife, embodying both mistress and spouse to comic effect. The remaining roles are divided between Actors 2 and 3, with the latter also stepping in to play one of the twins in the final scene.

Having one actor play both twins adds exciting comic dimensions to the script. It demands that the audience pay close attention to the actor's distinctions between them as well as the dramaturgical tricks required to pull off the illusion. Rambo (1915: 421) suggests, for example, that Menaechmus S always enters from one side of the stage (the direction of the harbour) while Menaechmus E enters from the opposite 'local' one (leading to downtown Epidamnus). This means that the actor regularly had to dash behind the scenes from one wing to the other, twice in the span of only about ten lines (216–225 and 558–570). Plautus dramatizes this technique in *Miles Gloriosus* when Philocomasium pretends to be her own twin, appearing from two separate houses via a hole in the wall between them. Having established this quick backstage movement as a recurring gag, is it is even more impressive when the actor must make an immediate exit and re-entrance at line 701. As Marshall (2006: 107) observes, 'Comic success in this context is achieved not by maintaining a seamless illusion about the separate identity of the characters, but by calling attention to the theatrical convention.' The audience knows it's an illusion and a big part of the fun is seeing how long the production can sustain the comic suspense and how it will eventually be resolved.

Masks, then, are the key to resolving the comic suspense and executing the recognition scene. Actor 3 takes over the role of

Menaechmus E at line 1050, simultaneously spotlighting and shattering the conceit the audience has been buying into all along. As Damen (1989: 417–18) observes, Plautus might have subbed in a mute actor, as Menander likely did at the end of *Dis Exapatōn*, or had the recognition scene occur offstage. Instead, two speaking twins appear onstage together in what Damen calls a 'satire of recognition scenes':

> By doing this, he directed his audience's attention to the impossibility of reuniting identical twins on stage, when one actor cannot play two parts at once and actors are not exactly identical. He also derived humor from a resolution which is not inherently humorous by emphasizing the ridiculousness not only of the characters' reactions but also the situation in the theatre. Far from Plautus' attempt to extract humor from what should be a cut-and-dry resolution, the extended recognition may be seen as a creative and comical solution to a problem inherent in Greek theatrical production.

The driving comic question of the play, then, is not 'will the brothers reunite in the end?' but rather 'how will the production pull off their impossible reunion?' The solution lies in the troupe's creative use of masks, the audience's willing suspension of disbelief, and a little dramaturgical magic.

c) Costumes

What did Roman comedic costumes look like? The truth is, we can't say for sure. While we have some tantalizing literary and artistic evidence, it combines to form a picture that is both incomplete and unreliable. Our literary evidence includes the plays themselves, a third-century CE dictionary by the Greek scholar Pollux (*Onomasticon*, 4.115-20), a fourth-century CE commentary by the Roman grammarian Donatus (*de comoedia*, 8.6-7), and brief references across the classical corpus, while the artistic evidence comprises illuminated manuscripts of Terence from the ninth century CE, as well as ancient wall paintings, reliefs and figurines. The Pollux, Donatus and Terence manuscripts are particularly enticing, but problematic. They are composed hundreds of years after the original productions of Plautus' plays and likely reflect later theatrical conventions. They also disagree in their details. As Duckworth (1952: 90) observes, in one Vatican manuscript the *senex* figure wears a bluish-white tunic and a yellow-brown pallium; in Donatus he wears all white. While in no way definitive, the extant sources can nonetheless give us a general idea of what the costumes may have looked like.[36]

A basic costume consisted of a tunic (*tunica*) and a cloak (*pallium* for men, *palla* for women). Comic padding was also available to simulate potbellies or pregnancies. Regardless of age or sex, all comic characters donned the same footwear: a thin sandal called the *soccus*, a distinctive feature of the genre.[37]

Young men and soldiers often wore a shorter cloak (*chlamys*), and accessories such as hats, belts or sabres. *Menaechmi* makes no explicit reference to the twins' clothing. The brothers may be dressed identically or distinguished by some signifier like a travel garment for Menaechmus S.[38] If they are dressed identically, it supports the ensuing confusion. If not, it undermines the misapprehension and adds visual comic layers to the performance.

Old men, like the wife's father, seem to have worn a long tunic with a *pallium* and might have carried a cane or a purse. Male slaves, like Messenio, often wore short tunics with long sleeves and a *pallium* or a scarf on their shoulder. In a stock gesture, the 'running slave' would toss the cloak over his shoulder and bustle about in a flurry of motion.[39] Women of all ages and social ranks (wives, slaves, courtesans) wore a long flowing tunic and a *palla* over their shoulders. As our play reveals, the same *palla* could be worn by a wife and a courtesan. Both characters could wear jewellery as well, such as the bracelet discussed at 524–558. Erotium's overall appearance, though, was likely more colourful and eye-catching than the *matrona's*, as befit her profession.

Parasites, like Peniculus, generally wore a long-sleeved tunic and are variously depicted in either a short *chlamys* or long *pallium*. Cooks, such as Cylindrus, appear in short, belted tunics holding kitchen supplies such as utensils and food items. As for the doctor, the *medicus* in *Menaechmi* is the only surviving example of this character type from Roman Comedy. A character dresses up as a doctor in Menander's *Aspis* (433–464) as part of a ruse, but there the disguise primarily functions as an accessory for satirizing foreign physicians. As Muecke (1987: 20) notes, without any concrete points of comparison, we can only 'conjecture that doctors were always figures of fun in comedy'.

d) Props

Both ancient and modern critics use the term 'props' interchangeably to refer to stage properties, costumes and set pieces. While closely related, these items serve discrete purposes in a play. Some distinction is therefore necessary. Let us follow Marshall (2006: 66–7) who defines props as 'those particular physical objects in a drama that create relationships: objects that are separable from their characters, the movement or transfer of which will be reflected in the dramatic action of the play'. He distinguishes them from objects that identify a given character (costumes) and objects that establish a performance space (sets).

Menaechmi expressly calls for an array of props: the cloak and bracelet that Menaechmus E steals from his wife and gives to Erotium, the garland that Menaechmus S wears upon his departure from Erotium's house, a shopping basket, money and groceries handled by Cylindrus, and baggage and a purse belonging to Menaechmus S. Each of these objects contributes in some way, large or small, to the mistaken identity set-up and helps the audience keep track of the titular twins.[40]

The most significant prop is undoubtedly the stolen cloak. Whether Menaechmus E is wearing the garment or simply carrying it when we first see him, it is a subject of spectacle (145). The *palla* serves a number of functions in the play: (1) it provides a cheap laugh when it is first introduced (a young man modelling women's clothing!), (2) it reveals that Menaechmus has been stealing from his wife, establishing the dysfunctional dynamic of their relationship, and (3) it serves as a key 'talisman', a marker that the audience tracks as it travels from the wife to Menaechmus E to Erotium to Menaechmus S and finally back to the wife again. Muecke (1987: 14) aptly applies the French philosopher Henri Bergson's theory of the 'talisman-farce' here, whereby 'mathematical permutations and combinations are anchored to reality by a physical object ("the talisman"), from which all confusions flow ... the talisman itself passes from hand to hand, tangling the lines of communication and generally spreading confusion between the characters'. The bracelet, too, plays a similar role.

The garland, first mentioned at line 463, also functions as a signifier that the audience (correctly) and the characters (incorrectly) use to identify a given twin. Peniculus sees Menaechmus S wearing it when he leaves Erotium's house and assumes his 'patron' has been revelling without him. This leads to their 'Mistaken Identity' confrontation. Menaechmus S tosses the garland aside at line 555, where it will rest undisturbed for 10 lines until it is found by the wife and parasite and taken as evidence of Menaechmus E's betrayal. When the real Menaechmus E returns from the forum shortly thereafter, without a garland, it confirms everyone's misapprehensions.

The remaining props – Cylindrus' shopping basket, money and groceries and Menaechmus S's baggage and a purse – are treated less prominently by the playwright, but serve similar functions. They signal one twin or the other and contextualize the ensuing confusion. Additionally, Plautus occasionally uses props to punctuate a joke, for example, when Messenio puns about Epidamnus' *damn*able reputation while discussing who will hold on to Menaechmus S's purse (263–264). Christenson's (2010: 54) excellent translation captures the comic spirit of these lines perfectly:

> It's a place for damnation, not a vacation (hence the name)!
> Drop in anytime – if you want to do some serious *dam*age to your wallet!

*

While at first sight *Menaechmi* might seem like a simple comedy of errors, it is well worth a double take. The play is steeped in the rich traditions of Greek and native Italian drama, it was vitally relevant to – and reflective of – its contemporary Roman culture, and it continues to speak to modern audiences and make us laugh. Plautus carefully calibrates the structure and pacing of the play to optimize the farcical fun, winding the mechanisms and sending the characters bouncing into one another with clockwork precision. His genius lies in his ability to make this complex multimodal activity appear spontaneous and effortless. What is more, he breathes new life into stock figures, playing with our expectations about their personalities and even the music that accompanies them. In the next chapter, we will examine the setting, characters and themes of *Menaechmi* in more detail, and explore how Plautus animates them with his distinctive style of humour.

2

Persons (and Places) of TWINterest: Setting, Characters and Themes

A Tale of Two Cities: Rome vs Epidamnus

While *Menaechmi* is nominally set in Epidamnus, it actually takes place in a fantasy world of Plautus' own design, a distillation and recombination of Generic Greece and Rome. Gratwick (1982: 113) famously dubs this world 'Plautinopolis'; its people, customs and landscape are simultaneously foreign and familiar, real and imaginary. It telescopes the distance between the reality of the audience and that of characters in the play. Plautus deliberately inserts Roman laws, customs, and even topography into the narrative, poking comically conspicuous holes in its Greek façade. In so doing, he invites his audience to reflect on and laugh at both Greek *and* Roman culture from a safe satirical distance.

The Prologue calls attention to the fluidity and flexibility of the setting right from the start. After welcoming the audience, he tells us that the story we're about to see takes place in the Greek(ish) world:

> Comic playwrights have this habit of pretending
> That everything on stage is taking place at Athens.
> Why? So you think it's in Greece, not Rome.
> Me? I won't pretend it takes place anywhere [*nusquam*] except where it
> happened.
> Yes indeed, this play will have a genuinely Greek atmosphere [*graecissat*],
> Though it's really more of a Sicilian air [*sicilicissitat*] than the aura of
> Athens [*atticissat*] about it.

7–12[1]

With this cheeky disclaimer, Plautus playfully, self-consciously, metatheatrically identifies *Menaechmi* as a typical Roman Comedy wherein the setting is all an illusion. As Moore (1998: 57) has observed, 'the *prologus' nusquam* ('nowhere') can mean either that the play occurred only where the *prologus* heard it did, or that it occurred nowhere at all. The jingling made-up verbs – inaccurate, since the play and most of the events leading up to the play do not occur in Sicily – reinforce this reminder that the Greek setting is a falsehood.' Indeed, even the characters don't seem to have a clear idea of where they are – at 231 Messenio incorrectly refers to Epidamnus as an island when, in fact, it is connected to the mainland by an isthmus.

If the setting is expressly fictive, a Graeco-Roman hybrid 'nowhere', why then did Plautus choose to identify it as 'Epidamnus'? The Prologue hints at the answer approximately midway through his speech:

> Now I must measure my way back to Epidamnus on foot [*pedibus*],
> To explain all of this to you down to the very last detail.
> If any one of you wants some *damned* [*Epidamnum*] business of yours
>   done there, speak up now.
> There's no need to fear as long as I'm taken care of –
> With cash up front, that is!
> No cash, you say? Well, you're screwed.
> Have the cash for me? See you later, then – and screw you!
> So let me go back to where I started, that is, right where I'm standing.
>   49–56

Revelling in wordplay, Plautus establishes two key points about the setting here. First, he reaffirms that his version of Epidamnus is a poetic fiction. It's the kind of place to which one can travel instantaneously . . . and on foot (*pedibus*), no less. He rounds out the joke with a metapoetic pun on *pedibus*, which can refer both to a mode of transport and also to the *metrical* feet, or units, of Latin verse. Secondly, Plautus names Epidamnus and discusses money-mismanagement in the same breath, closely associating the two. He combines the Greek preposition *epi* ('to', 'toward') and the Latin *damnum* ('financial loss') to engineer a bilingual pun that comes to define the city itself, underlining both its economic risks to the traveller and its fusion of Greece and Rome. As Franko (2009: 235) notes, 'while there is no discernible thematic reason for

Plautus to locate *Menaechmi* in Epidamnus, there is good sonic reason. Epidamnus provides ample opportunity for punning jokes'. This *damn* good pun becomes a running gag throughout the comedy, notably at 258–264:

> You do know about this damn nation of Epidamnians, don't you?
> Why it's decadence galore here! They've got loafers and slackers,
> Dipsomaniacs, kleptomaniacs, swindlers and chiselers everywhere!
> And surely you've heard about the local hookers?
> They're the most stunning *and* the most cunning in the world!
> It's a place for *damnation*, not a vacation (hence the name)!

The city's name is mentioned often and suggestively, conjuring the idea of a fantasy world populated by wicked women and scheming grifters. Epidamnus thus becomes a kind of character in and of itself. It is a space of revelry, mischief and dreamlike serendipity.[2] Shakespeare will build on this idea in his famous adaptation of the play, *The Comedy of Errors*, by characterizing his setting, Ephesus, as a place of magic and witchcraft (see chapter 4).

The Prologue concludes the *argumentum* with one final nod to the transience and theatricality of the setting:

> While this play is being staged, this city's [*haec urbs*] going to be
> Epidamnus;
> When it's time to stage another play, it'll be another town [*aliud oppidum*].
> The same thing happens with houses and households:
> One minute a pimp lives here, another minute a young man does.
> Or an old man, a pauper, a beggar, a king, a parasite, a fortune teller ...
>
> 72–76

With these words, the Prologue sends us off into the city (*haec urbs*), which will soon be another town (*aliud oppidum*), as generically anodyne as the character types who temporarily populate it. In so doing, he affirms the conventional nature of his comedy and sets a ludic tone that sanctions the tomfoolery about to ensue. The prologue of *Menaechmi* is Plautus' longest meditation on the theatricality of Roman

Comedy's Greek setting; it sums up his vision of 'Plautinopolis' here and across his corpus. The playwright blurs the boundaries between the Greek and Roman worlds in order to create an impermanent, inconsequential space where he is free to satirize the social conventions of both.

The most extensive example of this satirical boundary-blurring in our play occurs at 571–601, when Menaechmus E departs on a lengthy digression about the patron-client relationship. On his way back from the forum (yes, the *Roman* forum), he complains about the tedious responsibilities of being a patron and grumbles about being detained by a client who called him in to court to advocate on his behalf. Not only did he have to deal with the hassle of defending the many and terrible things his client did, but it also made him miss his lunch with Erotium! This thinly veiled reference to a distinctive Roman social convention in a distinctive Roman location stands out against the play's purported Greek backdrop. It provides the playwright with a perfect platform to mock the maddeningly moronic mores we [Romans] have (*Vt hoc utimur maxume more moro molesto atque multo,* 571–572). Gratwick (1993:193) calls this *canticum* 'one of the most explicitly "Roman" [Plautus] ever composed, and for us the earliest extensive comment on the enduring importance of *clientela* in Roman society'.

As we will see, the play is peppered with passing allusions to Roman customs and laws, from the marriage rights protecting the Wife's dowry to Messenio's manumission. The playwright casually weaves these into the fabric of 'Plautinopolis', simultaneously calling attention to local conventions and barbarizing them to comic effect.

The characters

The cast of characters who inhabit this metatheatrical Graeco-Roman-Epidamnian 'nowhere' represent a sample of the stock types whose traits and interactions exemplify New Comedy. While their faces may be familiar from one play to the next, Plautus refashions their features here, giving them fresh personalities uniquely suited to the plot and humour of *Menaechmi*.

a) The Prologue

A 'prologue' (lowercase p) is an introductory speech that generally precedes the main action of the play.[3] A 'Prologue' (capital P) is the figure who delivers this introductory speech. Three types of Prologues deliver the prologue in Plautus' plays: A main character who reappears elsewhere in the comedy (Mercurius in *Amphitruo*; Charinus in *Mercator*, and Palaestrio in *Miles Gloriosus*), a divine character that appears only once for this purpose (the Lar Familiaris in *Aulularia*, Auxilium in *Cistellaria*, Arcturus in *Rudens*, and Luxuria and Inopia in *Trinummus*), and, as we have here, an impersonal character, who has no other connection to the story (as also, *Asinaria, Captivi, Poenulus, Pseudolus, Truculentus* and *Vidularia*).

These figures serve two main functions: first, they introduce the play and lay out the plot summary (*argumentum*), if there is one, in order to make it as effortless as possible for the audience to follow.[4] This is particularly important in comedies of error like *Menaechmi* that revolve around mistaken identity, and that hinge on the audience's clear understanding of a situation alongside the characters' inability to grasp it. Our Prologue takes this job very seriously: 'Got it? Just so there's no confusion later, I repeat: BOTH BROTHERS HAVE THE SAME NAME' (*ne mox erratis, iam nunc praedico prius: idem est ambobus nomen geminis fratribus*, 47–48). Secondly, and perhaps most importantly, Prologues 'warm up' the audience, establishing a breezy, affable rapport between the stage-folk and the spectators. They often solicit the audience's favour outright, for example, when our Prologue says: 'I only ask that you and your ears be kind to this play and give it a fair hearing' (3). They also poke fun at actors and audience members alike, forging a banter-based bond between them, as when our Prologue calls attention to the audience's foolishness in both giving and not giving him money (54–55). This joke seems to have been a particularly popular one – Plautus has the Prologue repeat it in *Poenulus* (81–82). In this way, this figure plays a key role in setting a congenial comic tone.

Menaechmi offers us a paragon of a Prologue. His is a minor, but scene-stealing role. He cracks metatheatrical jokes, delivers silly puns, and untangles a densely knotted back-story. As Gratwick (1993: 33–4) observes, 'his dramatic identity is interesting as a study in ambiguity, the very essence of Plautine Comedy. For he is and is not the playwright, the impresario, the magistrate, an actor, a stand-up comedian, one of us, and a salesman who plays on our gullibility to make us believe in *quod fit nusquam*; a plausible liar conjuring up a festive comic world – Plaut[in]opolis.' He is impersonal, but immensely personable, and he shoulders the important responsibility of capturing the audience's attention right from the start and shaping their first impressions of the play.

b) The young men

The name 'Menaechmus' recalls the Greek word *menaichmos*, meaning 'staunch soldier'.[5] It might be a portmanteau of the Greek words *meno* ('remain') and *aichme* ('point' or 'cusp'), highlighting the brothers' liminal position on the cusp of fortune.[6] Plautus may have invented the name from scratch or he may have adapted it from the fourth-century mathematician and geometer from Syracuse of the same name, who – appropriately enough – solved the problem of 'doubling the cube'.[7] Either way, the name, like 'Sosicles', is meant to sound highfalutin, heroic and *Greek*.

The titular twins who share this name fall under the stock category of the 'young man' (*adulescens*). This figure is typically the lover around whose amorous pursuits the plot revolves. His personal freedom is often limited by paternal authority or lack of money, and he regularly requires the help of a clever slave to win his beloved. In terms of personality, he has a kind of quirky charm: the *adulescens* is clueless, but earnest; vapid, but enthusiastic. Gratwick (1982: 107) calls the young man 'the most schizophrenic of Plautus' characters. His ruling humour as lover is *immodestia*, a lack of a sense of proportion . . . . The reason is that he is in love, a self-sufficient excuse for anything, for love is represented not as Plato's divine madness but plain if amiable lunacy.'

While Menaechmus E and Menaechmus S are technically *adulescentes* by virtue of their age and sex, they also depart from the type. They fit the mould in that they are both foolish lovers of Erotium and they rely on Messenio's help to resolve their confusion in the final recognition scene. However, neither one is subject to a father's control, both are independently wealthy, and the plot centres around one twin's quest to find the other, rather than a love story. Another anomaly is that Menaechmus E is already married. As Muecke (1987: 16) has observed, he is the only young 'adulterer' of extant New Comedy. While the fact that he is already married does make him seem somewhat older than the typical Plautine *adulescens*, his mask – and his behaviour! – underscore his immaturity.

While the twins are identical in appearance, they differ in personality. Menaechmus E shows his true colours the moment he enters the stage, shouting at his spouse, bragging about his infidelity, exulting in his larceny, and dressed in drag, modelling the *palla* that he stole from his wife to give his mistress. He is the fool for love who is accompanied by music whenever he appears.[8] Embodying the Saturnalian spirit of comedy, the *adulescens* indulges in what Segal (2001: 118–24) refers to as the Pleasure Principle, that is, the playful 'holiday psychology' that rebels against the responsible restrictions of everyday life.

By contrast, Menaechmus S makes a sober first impression, assuredly stepping onshore after years at sea searching for his brother, nobly vowing: 'I'll never stop looking for him as long as I'm breathing. I'm the only one who understands the place he holds in my heart' (245–246). He is the serious *adulescens*, who gradually relinquishes more and more of his self-control as the play progresses and he begins to live his brother's life. Left to his own devices in this Epi*damn*ed city, he gradually devolves into the worst version of himself, surrendering to one temptation after another and exploiting strangers. And because *he* has no relationship with Menaechmus E's wife, mistress, parasite, etc., he is free to say whatever he wants to them. As Segal (2001: 116) observes, he is 'a surrogate self, the alter ego with no superego, someone who can indulge his appetite for pleasure without concern for the consequences'. Falling under Epidamnus' spell, Menaechmus S becomes more and more like his twin until, at last, in the final scene he too enters to continued musical accompaniment. The Menaechmi brothers thus provide vivid examples of how Plautus individualizes stock characters from one comedy to the next and even within the same play.

c) The slaves

According to Roman law, slaves were property, not people. They had no legal rights, no social standing, no independent identities, no autonomous voices. They were subject to frequent and arbitrary physical violence, emotional abuse and sexual exploitation. They were victims of horrific and indiscriminate circumstance: war captivity, kidnapping, human trafficking, extreme poverty. The ludic licence that slaves often enjoy in comedy bears little resemblance to the tragedy of their lived experience.[9]

The spectre of slavery haunted every aspect of Roman Comedy: many actors were slaves themselves, slave characters were prominently featured on the stage, real-life slaves sat in the audience alongside their masters, and the (mis)fortune of slaves was a frequent subject of dramatic discourse. There is at least one principal slave character in every extant Roman Comedy, and often an ensemble of slaves plays minor roles as well (e.g. household slaves, prostitutes, maids, pages, porters and entertainers). *Menaechmi* showcases a good number of them: Messenio (*servus*), Erotium's unnamed maid (*ancilla*), and Cylindrus (*coquus*), along with an indeterminate number of (mostly) mute attendants who accompany Menaechmus S, Erotium, the Old Man and the Wife. Since the cook is a specialized slave role, we will examine him in his own section shortly. For now, let us focus on the archetypal slaves: Messenio, Erotium's unnamed maid, and the voiceless attendants.

The slave (*servus*) in Roman Comedy is typically the young man's loyal sidekick, partner in crime, and often the brains behind the operation. Gratwick (1982: 106–7) neatly encapsulates this figure as follows:

> He is *doctus* 'clever', *astutus* 'sophisticated', *malus* 'bad', *nequam* 'good for nothing', and is given to self-glorification, arrogating to himself the status and rights of a citizen, reversing roles with his betters and giving the orders, and, as master-builder and military expert, comparing his exploits and strategy with those of kings and epic heroes. The slave is the most internally consistent of Plautus' types, and he has the power to address the audience confidentially without disrupting the dramatic illusion. He is at once a member of the audience and of the cast, the director of the action, and the intermediary between us and the more exotic characters. There is, as it were, no actor behind the mask of the slave.

Messenio is a variation on the clever slave type (*servus callidus*). His name means 'a person from Messene', a Greek community in the Peloponnese, known for its subjugated class of helots controlled by Sparta. This onomastic form (i.e. a name based on a country of origin) is typical for a slave. Messenio is not a cunning trickster like some of Plautus' splashier slaves, who concoct elaborate schemes to help their masters win the day (e.g. Chrysalus in *Bacchides*, Palaestrio in *Miles Gloriosus*, Toxilus in *Persa*, Milphio in *Poenulus*, and, of course, Pseudolus in *Pseudolus*). Messenio is practical, cautious, and his master's moral compass, especially early on in the story before Menaechmus S gets swept up in his brother's shenanigans. In short, he plays the straight-man to his master's fool. At the same time, he possesses the two most salient characteristics of comedic *servi callidi*: intelligence and outspokenness. With regard to intelligence, Messenio is much sharper than his master, solving the mystery of the mistaken identities well before he does and leveraging it for his freedom: 'Immortal gods! Am I looking at what I've looked forward to for so long? Unless I'm mistaken, these two are identical twins! And according to their stories, they were fathered by the same father and hail from the same country! I'll call my master aside! Menaechmus!' (1081–1084).

With regard to outspokenness, Messenio openly opines and challenges his master on a number of occasions, notably in their first scene together. When Menaechmus S announces that they've come to Epidamnus to find his long-lost twin brother, Messenio gripes: 'You're looking for a peck of pears on an elm tree. We should just go back home – unless we're planning to write a travelogue' (247–248). Menaechmus S is quick to put him in his place: 'Do what you're told, eat what you're given, watch out for trouble. Stop bothering me: it's my way or the highway' (249–250). With a shrug to the audience, Messenio concedes his lot: 'Ouch! That's cutting to the chase! Okay, I'M A SLAVE [*esse me servom scio*]. No one's ever said that so loudly and clearly before, and in so few words! But I won't bite my tongue about one thing [*verum tamen nequeo contineri quin loquar* ...]' (251–253). This early dialogue between Messenio and Menaechmus S reveals how their comic relationship pushes – but remains safely within – the boundaries of the normative master-slave dynamic.

Plautus brings the subject of slavery centre-stage when he gives Messenio a show-stopping musical number on the topic (966–989). Alone in the (figurative) spotlight, Messenio meditates on the proper character and conduct of a 'good' slave and reflects on the grisly punishments in store for a 'bad' one:

> *This is the trademark of a good slave: his eyes are fixed*
> *On his master's affairs (watching, gauging, arranging them*
> *So that when his Master's away, his orders still hold sway)*
> *And then some, just as if he were there.*
> *A slave with horse-sense respects his back more than his craw,*
> *His shanks more than his belly.*
> *And he must always be mindful of what masters*
> *Mete out to wicked and worthless slaves:*
> *Whips, chains*
> *Millstones, fatigue, famine, piercing frost –*
> *These are the wages of slacking!*
> *This is just the sort of trouble I take pains to escape: ergo, I'll be good, not*
> *bad this time.*

*I can stand a tongue-lashing [verba], but my back just can't hack that
type of treatment [verbera].*
I like my bread ground, but I'd rather not be part of that grind!
That's why I follow Master's orders calmly and carefully,
That's what works best for me.
Others can do as they think is best for them; I'll be as I ought to be.
That's my rule: to be blameless and always at Master's beck and call.
The best slaves are afraid of their masters even when they've nothing to fear.
*Those who don't fear them, become afraid too late – after a well-deserved
beating!*
*Since their masters mete out punishment, that kind of fear doesn't really
work for them.*
My service is dedicated to the principle of doing what's best for my back.
*I checked the luggage and the slaves into the inn, just as Master ordered,
And I've come here to meet him. I'll knock on the door to tell him I'm
present,*
And guide my Master out safely from this forest of evil.
But I'm afraid I've come too late – and the battle's over.

966–989

The catalogue of cruelty (whips, chains, millstones, fatigue, famine,
piercing frost) quickly snowballs into bleak hyperbole, leaning into the
darker side of Plautus' sense of humour. Ever the pragmatist, Messenio
admits that his behaviour is equally motivated by fear of punishment as
hope for reward. With typical Plautine wordplay, he hopes for *verba*
(reprimands) rather than *verbera* (beatings, 978). He declares his
intentions to keep his head down and his person safe, a theme that
Plautus revisits in Phaniscus' speech at *Mostellaria* 858–884. The
underlying pessimism – a 'bad' slave will always pay the price – shatters
the comic conceit and drops the dramatic illusion for a heartbreakingly
real moment wherein the audience is invited to consider what life is
really like for a slave off of the stage. In this tragicomic way, Messenio
gives a voice to a voiceless population. Gratwick (1993: 227) and others
generally agree that Plautus added this *canticum* in his reworking of the
Greek original. In addition to justifying Messenio's presence onstage
before the fight scene, the song provides a platform for the playwright

to address a dominant theme in the play and in Roman Comedy more broadly.

Despite the precarious nature of the master-slave relationship, Messenio seems to legitimately care for Menaechmus S. His devotion to his master is on full display in the fight scene (997–1020), when he valiantly leaps into the fray without a second thought for his own safety. After fending off the assailants, he asks his 'master' for his freedom in exchange for this act of bravery and loyalty. Menaechmus E, of course, has no connection to Messenio and accordingly replies 'by god, as far as I'm concerned, you can go wherever you like and be free' (*mea quidem hercle causa liber esto atque ito quo voles*, 1029). With these procedural words (*liber esto*), the Epidamnian twin unwittingly frees the slave. Messenio rejoices; he underscores his genuine affection for his 'master' when he requests to stay with him and remain in his service as a client, a common practice of freedmen in Rome. It is all the more poignant, then, when Menaechmus S, ignorant of Messenio's exchange with his brother, reneges on the promise of his freedom: 'Yeah? Well I most definitely would sooner become a slave myself than emancipate you!' (1058–1059). The story is hurtling toward its resolution, however, and the slave will play a key role in masterminding the finale. Applying his superior intellect, Messenio cracks the case of the Mistaken Identities and negotiates his knowledge for his freedom. Plautus thus ties the comedy's happy ending together with that of the slave. In this deliberate and meaningful way, Plautus effectively makes Messenio the most heroic, intelligent and sympathetic character in *Menaechmi*.

Erotium's unnamed maid presents another comic portrait of a slave. Stripped of her identity, she is referred to only as *ancilla*, meaning 'female slave'. She shares a brief scene with Menaechmus S at 524–558 as he leaves Erotium's house with the *palla* in hand. Mistaking him for his brother, she gives him a bracelet (*spinter*) to take the jeweller on behalf of her mistress. She casually mentions how he stole from his wife (again) and shamelessly flirts with him in hopes of snagging some gold earrings for herself: 'And Menaechmus, do be a dear and get me some earrings – pendants, made of four drachmas worth of gold. I'd be so happy to see you the next time you came to visit our house' (541–543). Menaechmus S has no idea who all these women are and why they keep giving him expensive apparel, but he decides not to question his good fortune. Lowe (2019: 8) among others, regards this short 'add-on' scene as another Plautine innovation to the Greek original. It introduces a second 'talisman' for the audience to keep track of – the *spinter*, in addition to the *palla* –but otherwise it does not move the plot forward in any meaningful way. Of note: the *ancilla* and the doctor are the only figures from Epidamnus who interact solely with the Syracusan twin. All of the other characters from Menaechmus E's world – Peniculus, Erotium, Cylindrus, the Wife, the Old Man – share at least one scene with both brothers, contributing to the escalating confusion over mistaken identity. The sole purpose of the ancilla's and the doctor's cameos is to showcase a stock character doing their stock shtick. In the case of the *ancilla*, her cameo provides an opportunity for comic banter between a sassy *ancilla* and a foolish *adulescens*. Indeed, as a counterpart to the *servus callidus*, the *ancilla's* most common function in Roman Comedy is to be a witty and shrewd foil for higher status characters.

Several other slave figures bustle around the background of *Menaechmi* as (mostly) mute extras, adding colour, movement and energy to the scenes in which they appear. Because they generally have no lines, it is easy to overlook their presence on the page. They make a striking impression on the stage, however, animating and amplifying the spectacle unfolding before the audience's eyes.[10] In our play, these (mostly) mute extras include: the porters who carry Menaechmus S's baggage (225–445), the Wife's maid 'Deceo' (736), the Old Man's attendants who attack Menaechmus E (990–1018), and possibly additional maids to Erotium and to the Wife. Identifying and keeping track of their presence in the script requires a bit of detective work: The porters, for example, are onstage for approximately 125 lines before they're first addressed by Messenio. This lack of recognition arguably reinforces their low social status; the first and last we hear of them is by way of someone's orders. At line 350, Messenio calls them 'Nautical Feet' (*navales pedes*) and tells them to keep an eye on their belongings. They remain onstage throughout Menaechmus S and Messenio's early scenes with Cylindrus and Erotium, and only depart when Menaechmus S tells Messenio to take them to the inn at 436. What are they doing all that time?

Perhaps they perform a comical pantomime upon entering, bumping into one another and bumbling around with the baggage. Perhaps they mimetically mock Cylindrus as he fumbles his way through the first Mistaken Identity Bit. Perhaps they silently, but conspicuously judge their master for blindly leaping into Erotium's arms. Perhaps they drool over her themselves like Tex Avery cartoon wolves. While it's impossible to definitively reconstruct their original body language, one can imagine a wide range of creative possibilities and the exciting dramatic effects they might have had. These characters communicate entirely through gesture, which can either complement or contradict the dialogue spoken to and around them.

The most prominent figures of this type in our play are the Old Man's slaves who assault Menaechmus E at 996–1018. There are probably at least four of them; at 953, the doctor recommends this as the minimum number required to restrain the madman. Once again, their presence is acknowledged by way of orders; the *senex* commands them to capture Menaechmus E and bring him to the *medicus'* house for observation. Typical of master-slave dialogue, he threatens them with physical violence if they don't obey. Of course, if they follow his orders, they'll meet with a violent fate all the same. They're Epi*damn*ed if they do, and Epi*damn*ed if they don't:

> By heaven and earth, you need to follow all my orders, to the letter,
> Both the ones I've given you and the ones I'm giving you now.
> Now pick that man up and carry him off to the doctor's house,
> Unless you don't give a rat's ass for your shanks and flanks!
> And don't pay the least bit of attention to any of his threats.
> *Don't stand there! You should have already picked him up.*
> *I'm off to the Doctor's. I'll meet you there when you arrive*

990–996

This scene no doubt involved dynamic fight choreography underscored by lively musical accompaniment. The dialogue reveals hints about the staging:

> **Menaechmus [E]**   *Now I'm dead!*
> *What's going on? Why in the world are these men rushing at me?*
> *What is it you want from me? Why are you all surrounding me?*
> *What's the big rush? Hey, where are you taking me? I'm done for!*
> *Help, citizens of Epidamnus, help me! Hey, let go of me!*
> **Messenio**   *By the almighty gods! I can hardly believe my own eyes!*
> *Some strangers are carrying off Master as if he's a criminal!*
>
> 997–1002

With over-the-top running commentary, Messenio encourages his 'master' to 'rip out the eye of that guy who has you by the shoulder' (1011) and proclaims that he will 'plant his fists all over their faces' (1012). Menaechmus E shouts, 'I've got this one's eye', to which Messenio responds 'Keep a hold on it 'til the socket shows!' (1014). The more graphic the play-by-plays, the higher the comedic stakes. And, of course, since this is stage violence without any real-world consequence, the audience is free to enjoy the acrobatics and laugh at the hullaballoo without fear for the actual well-being of any of the parties involved.

At 1015, Messenio deals a blow to three of the pugilists in quick succession: 'you … you … you …' (*vos … vos … vos …*). At this point, one of the otherwise mute slaves is given a single line: 'We're dead! Please help!' (*periimus! Obsecro hercle!*, 1015–1016). This plea to the audience is all the more striking in light of the characters' silence up until this point. By giving the slaves one line – and a cry for help at that – Plautus inserts moving social commentary into this farcically belligerent ballet. The (mostly) mute characters thus serve a number of key functions in *Menaechmi*. They are valuable agents of visual gags, physical comedy and improvisation, all of which are fundamental elements of the genre. Additionally, as predominately subaltern, marginalized figures, they cast a spotlight onto the shadowy roles that slaves play, both on and off the stage.

d) The prostitute

Erotium's name, a diminutive form of the Greek word *eros* ('Little Love'; 'Lovey-Wuvy'), befits her profession. She is a prostitute (*meretrix*) and, as such, a lightning rod and fringe figure of both fascination and disdain in Roman society. Prostitution was legal in ancient Rome, but mediated by its honour-shame culture. McGinn (2003: 17) contextualizes the social function of prostitution in the time of Plautus and extending to the early empire of the first century CE as follows:

> Uncontrolled sexuality, represented above all by adultery, posed a threat to the moral and political order. Prostitution played an important role in safeguarding this order. Though part of a disgraced milieu that embraced the lowest orders of society, it complemented the respectable aspect, which in sexual and reproductive terms meant marriage and the rearing of children. It functioned in this way for males by distracting potential predators from women whose honor was deemed worth preserving and for females by serving as a warning of the consequences should sexual honor be lost. Prostitution—disgraced but tolerated—formed a licit area of Roman sexuality and enjoyed an ambivalent status rendered the more nuanced after the introduction of the Augustan legislation on sex and marriage and the Caligulan tax on prostitution, the latter of which contributed a certain degree of legitimacy to its practice.

Prostitutes – like other 'entertainment' figures such as gladiators and actors – were considered shameful (*infames; infamis* in the singular). They were socially marginalized and subject to a host of religious, political and civic disabilities, including exclusion from certain cult practices and denial of basic legal rights.[11] Compounding their lowly social status was the fact that most *meretrices* were either slaves or freedwomen.

Slave *meretrices* had to endure the merciless authority of pimps, who were *infames* themselves and popular villains of Roman Comedy. Freedwomen, like Erotium, enjoyed more independence and could even own their own establishments, supporting themselves through the patronage of their clients. Their (im)pure economic motives, however, further tarnished their reputations and shaped the way they were caricatured in the public imagination and on the Roman stage.

Duckworth (1952: 258) notes that 'the courtesans of Plautus fall into two categories: (1) the ones who are clever and experienced but mercenary and unfeeling; (2) younger girls who, devoted to their lovers, have already become their mistresses or who are hoping to be purchased and freed. To those of the first group money rather than love is a determining factor in the bestowal of their favors.' Marshall (2013: 174–9) observes that this distinction also correlates with the *meretrix's* social status: Non-citizen, but free *meretrices* are more likely to fall into the former category than enslaved ones. Erotium is a textbook example of this first type, as evidenced by her response to Menaechmus E when he gifts her the *palla*: 'You're the best! You outrank all the other johns who want to infiltrate my unit' (*superas facile ut superior sis mihi quam quisquam qui imperant*, 192). She joins the Bacchis Sisters (*Bacchides*), Phronesium (*Truculentus*) and Acroteleutium (*Miles Gloriosus*) in Plautus' pantheon of pragmatic prostitutes. As Gratwick (1982: 110) remarks, this figure is 'exotic, extravagant, and amoral rather than immoral. She is presented as the intellectual equal of the clever slave, being *docta, astuta, callida, faceta, mala, nequam*, and taking the same detached views of love as he.' Erotium's impersonal, all-business approach to love renders her name all the more ironic.

Indeed, the *meretrix* manipulates Menaechmus from the very first moment she steps onto the stage: 'Menaechmus! Hello, dearest darling!' (*anime, mi Menaechme, salve*, 182). Even Peniculus, a fellow flatterer, has to admire her work: 'Aw, there's nothing sweeter than a prostitute with a target in her sights' (*meretrix tantisper blanditur, dum illud quod rapiat videt*, 193). She continues to lay it on thick, even when addressing the wrong brother at 370–372: 'My goodness! You're well aware it's Venus' will that I adore you beyond all my other lovers. And you certainly deserve it, seeing that I flourish because of you and your gifts alone!' Erotium is a consummate professional; she knows exactly what to say and do to get her way. She even lays out precise instructions to her slaves on how to prepare for the banquet, effectively outlining her strategy for seduction (in song!):

Leave the doors open, just as they are. Go back in,
See everything's done that needs to be done.
Deck out the couches, fire up the incense:
Elegance lures and entices a lover's heart.
Our charm brings them pain – and us gain!
But where is he? The cook said he was out by the door. Oh, he's over there:
My finest and foremost source of income!
As long as his cash keeps pouring in, he reigns supreme in this house!

                                                                351–359

Menaechmus E is happily ignorant of Erotium's agenda. He's fallen for her act, hook, line and sinker, swooning: 'you're the only woman in the world who knows what I like' (202). His brother is more skeptical . . . at least in the beginning: 'I'll know soon enough whether it's me or the wallet she wants' (386). As Christenson (2010: 13) remarks, 'the true superficiality of Menaechmus [E]'s purely economic relationship with Erotium is best captured when . . . she has an intimate lunch followed by sex with the drastically different Menaechmus [S] without ever suspecting that he is not Menaechmus [E]'.

At the same time, Erotium is not all sweet-talk and seduction. She assertively voices her frustration with Menaechmus E when he returns to her house after his confrontation with his wife and asks her to return the *palla*, which she's already given to his brother. Fed up with his foolishness, Erotium kicks him out and dictates the revised terms of the relationship moving forward:

Well, I didn't even ask you for it in the first place.
You brought *it* to *me* on your own. You told me it was a present for me
And now you're asking for it back. Fine. Take it, keep it, wear it as you
    please,
Or let your wife wear it! You can lock it away in a vault for all I care.
And make no mistake about it: you'll never step foot in this house again!
After all I've done for you, you treat me with such contempt!

> Unless you come with lots of cash, your days of having fun with me are
> over
>
>   688–695

Erotium thus sends Menaechmus E moping off into the mean streets of Epidamnus. McCarthy (2000: 37) notes that, in theory, the nature of the *adulescens-meretrix* relationship should be 'purely economic without the complex entanglements of emotion and decorum'. Once they inevitably get involved, however, it is Erotium who calls things off with her lover. In this way, we can see the subversive power dynamics at play in their relationship. On the one hand, according to Roman culture, Erotium is Menaechmus' subordinate with respect to her profession, her social status, and her gender. On the other hand, she enjoys complete control over him, securing his affection, money and gifts by means of her feminine wiles. In Erotium's case – and more broadly with the prostitutes of Roman Comedy – it is not always clear who is exploiting whom.

e) The cook

Cylindrus' name means 'cylinder', 'roller' or 'rolling pin' in Greek; it effectively announces his identity as a cook (*coquus*). Plautus underlines the culinary wordplay at 294–295: 'Cylindrus: I'm Cylindrus! You know my name, don't you? Menaechmus S: I don't care if you're Cylinder or Coriander – I just want you to get lost!' (*Cylindrus ego sum: non nosti nomen meum? si tu Cylindrus seu Coriendru's, perieris*). A descendant of Greek Middle and New Comedy, he is one of a long line of comic cooks who stir up commotion on the Plautine stage (cf. *Mercator* 741–782, *Aulularia* 280–459, *Pseudolus* 790–895, *Truculentus* 551–630, *Miles Gloriosus* 1394–1427, *Curculio* 251–370, *Casina* 720–748 and *Bacchides* 109–169). Cooks in Plautus are figures of great fun: they are almost always loud, often proud, and occasionally sticky-fingered. Like their fellow comic slaves, the *servi callidi*, they tend to be quite talkative and call things as they see them. They are also capable agents of physical comedy. They can raise hilarious ruckuses onstage (mis)handling their props, whether banging on pots and pans or lugging baskets of provisions for a feast.

Cylindrus arrives on the scene at 219, when Erotium briefly summons him onstage before sending him off to the market to buy food for the banquet. He returns home again at 273, where he runs into Menaechmus S and Messenio. He has the distinct honour of being the first character they meet in Epidamnus and the first unwitting participant in the chain of Mistaken Identity Bits that ensue. As Lowe (1985: 90) observes, 'Confusion inevitably results, and this is Cylindrus' dramatic *raison d'être*; after this scene he does not appear again, although we hear more of his lunch in Erotium's house.' Lowe (1985: 90–2) posits that this character was likely a fixture from the Greek original of the Roman Comedy, but that in the original he was probably just an ordinary household slave. His dramatic function here doesn't actually require him to be a cook, though his interactions with both Erotium and Menaechmus S and Messenio are integral to developing the plot and the theme of Mistaken Identity. Lowe suggests that Plautus deliberately chose to make Cylindrus a *coquus* rather than a *servus* in order to give the role some 'extra colour'.

Indeed, Cylindrus does contribute a colourful comic cameo. He has a number of witty one-liners, for example, when he inquires about the guest list for the banquet and impertinently opines that Peniculus eats as much as eight people (223). He also shakes up the tone of the dialogue by mixing in some tragic grandiloquence: 'And you should just go ... straight in and take your place at the table while these victuals wend their way to Vulcan's violence' (*ire hercle meliust te ... interim atque accumbere, dum ego haec appono ad Volcani uiolentiam*, 329–330). Like any comic cook worth his salt, Cylindrus adds zest to the scenes in which he appears.

f) The parasite

The parasite (*parasitus*) is the first main character we meet, following the expository prologue. He immediately and directly addresses the audience, establishing a personal relationship with them that will run parallel to the dramatic narrative in all of his scenes. He will share several monologues and asides with the audience over the course of the play, giving them an 'insider' view of the story and cementing an alliance with them, whatever they may think of his character flaws, this metatheatrical dynamic is a key part of the parasite's power and appeal in Roman Comedy (see chapter 3).

He sets a comic tone right away, just by introducing himself as Peniculus. Since the word is a diminutive form of the Latin *'penis'* ('Little Dick'), he seems to be setting up a sexual joke (Cf. Ergasilus' entrance at *Captivi* 69). He quickly subverts the audience's expectations by explaining that his nickname derives from the word's *other* meaning, 'sponge' or 'brush' ... 'because he always wipes the dinner table clean' (*iuuentus nomen fecit Peniculo mihi, ideo quia ... mensam quando edo detergeo*, 77–78). In this way he impishly, unabashedly self-identifies as a parasite.

Duckworth (1952: 265) calls the parasite 'the "funny" man *par excellence* of Roman Comedy'. The parasite is an unapologetic glutton who will happily humiliate himself in order to satisfy his comically insatiable appetite. This usually involves fawning over a boorish patron, who exchanges food for false flattery. Damon (1997: 98–9) neatly summarizes his salient characteristics as follows: 'The parasite can be sketched with a few essential traits: he ranks food as his *summum bonum*, he is unable (through situation or temperament) to provide it for himself but is clever enough to extract it from others, and he lacks the pride and principles that ought to characterize a man of his free status.'

Peniculus' first monologue (77–109) paints a vivid portrait of the parasite. He meditates on man's enslavement to his appetite, likening food to the chains that bind a slave to his master. Like similar monologues delivered by fellow Plautine parasites in *Captivi, Persa* and *Stichus,* he both comments upon and embodies the conventional qualities of this stock character. As McCarthy (2000: 63) observes, the 'most distinctive element of these speeches is the way they are so emphatically focused on the description of the "trade" of parasitism itself. There are parallels in the corpus, but no other character type is so pervasively associated with such a distinctive subject matter and expression.' A self-aware, metatheatrical figure, the parasite playfully stretches the limits of the dramatic illusion:

> Why, what's the right and proper way to keep a man from fleeing?
> Why, chains of food and drink of course!
> Let him clamp his jaws down on a full table,
> Keep serving him his favorite edibles and potables each and every day,
> And you'll wear him down with satisfaction.
> He'll never escape, not even if he's facing capital punishment.
> It's really that simple. There's no stronger chain
> Than the food-chain: the looser you let it out,
> The tighter it ties a criminal down.
> Case in point: myself. I'm off to Menaechmus' house here,
> Where I've been a prisoner for years. Bring on the chains, yum, yum!
>
> 87–97

With refreshing candour, Peniculus explains exactly why it is he keeps company with Menaechmus E. He praises his patron, not for the content of his character, but for the extravagance of the banquets that he throws: 'That's the type of young man he is. He serves feasts fit for Ceres, his helpings are huge, veritable mountains of food! He concocts culinary monuments so lofty, you have to stand on your couch to trim a tasty morsel off the summit!' (100–103). His empty larder is what brings him to Menaechmus E's door that day. Peniculus may be a lowly parasite, but, along with Messenio, he is one of the most honest, self-reflective characters in the play.

When Menaechmus E first enters, railing at his wife, Peniculus shares an aside with the audience before even greeting his patron. In so doing, he prioritizes his relationship with them: 'He may think he's bad-mouthing his wife, but I'm the one taking it in the jaw. If he dines out, he punishes my stomach, not his wife' (125–126). The parasite's wry commentary here and throughout the play bolsters his connection with the audience. They bond with one another over a shared sense of knowingness over the fools onstage.

Menaechmus E is delighted to see Peniculus. Exulting in his theft of the *palla* and excited about his imminent visit to Erotium, the *adulescens* is eager for a sympathetic audience and a co-conspirator, and Peniculus is just the parasite for the job. Food is never far from Peniculus' mind, however, and he is quick to remind his patron that his flattery comes at a price:

Menaechmus [E] Check this out: Remind you of anything (*models the pashmina*)?

Peniculus What's with the get-up?

Menaechmus [E] Aren't I just the most charming fellow (*homo lepidissume*) you've ever seen?

Peniculus When's dinner?

Menaechmus [E] Didn't I just ask you a question?

Peniculus Yes, yes, you're the most charming fellow (*homo lepidissume*) ever.

Menaechmus [E] And? Anything else?

Peniculus Yeah. You're a hoot. Absolutely hilarious.

Menaechmus [E] And?

Peniculus Please, no more 'And?'s! . . . until I know what's in it for me. You and your wife are back at it again. All the more reason to watch my back.

Menaechmus [E] We're going to seize the day and burn it right up in a place my wife doesn't know about.

Peniculus Oh, well put! So how soon do I light the pyre? The day's already half-dead-right down to its belly-button.

146–155

The parasite's toadyism is on full display here, but his lack of enthusiasm for Menaechmus' mischief is such that he can't even come up his own words of praise. Instead he just parrots his patron ('the most charming fellow', *homo lepidissume*) and says what he needs to in order to secure an invitation to the afternoon's festivities. His patron is either blissfully ignorant of his cynicism or he willingly turns a blind eye to it.

Menaechmus E is similarly oblivious to the *meretrix*'s manipulation when they arrive at the prostitute's house next door. In fact, Peniculus has a lot in common with Erotium. As McCarthy (2000: 63) observes, their main skill-set – and indeed their defining characteristic – is their 'ability to perceive and make use of what Menaechmus would like to hear'. She goes on to note, however, that the audience's reception of these characters is very different, since Peniculus occupies a privileged metatheatrical position where he can comment on Erotium's actions and mediate how she will be perceived. It is for this reason that the parasite is ultimately a more sympathetic character.

Peniculus leaves for the forum with Menaechmus E at 216 and doesn't reappear until 446. Upon his return, he immediately confides in the audience once again, complaining about getting tied up in a public meeting and becoming separated from his patron. Hungrier than ever, he hopes he's made it back in time for the banquet. When he sees Menaechmus S wearing a garland and departing from Erotium's house, he assumes the worst: that his patron intentionally brushed him off in order to party with his prostitute without him! He vows vengeance: 'By Hercules, I'm not the man that I am (*non hercle <ego> is sum qui sum*), if I don't avenge this injustice with sweet, sweet revenge. Oh, just watch me, you!' (471–472). With a curse that ironically plays on the theme of identity, Peniculus' outsized outrage heightens the comic energy going into the next Mistaken Identity Bit. For a normal human being, the magnitude of his anger would be wildly disproportionate to the minor scale of the offence, but for a parasite, well, failing to honor the promise of a hard-earned meal is the *ultimate* insult:

> You irresponsible airhead!
> You utterly foul and worthless person! You disgrace to the human race!
> You disgusting cheater! Just what do you have to say for yourself?
> What did I ever do to make you want to destroy me?
> First you sneak away from me at the forum!
> Then you devour lunch without me even there to give it a decent burial!
> I was just as much its heir as you were! How could you?
>
> 487–493

Peniculus is already so worked up that when Menaechmus S claims not to know him, he all but explodes. The parasite storms away, swearing that his patron will be sorry ... for eating his lunch! (521). He will tell Menaechmus E's wife everything he knows. This, of course, means nothing to Menaechmus S, but as far as the audience is concerned, he is detonating the comedic equivalent of a nuclear bomb. Peniculus' most important function here is to raise the dramatic tension to its breaking point heading into the showdown with the *matrona*.

The parasite returns onstage with the furious wife at 559. They position themselves off to the side where they can fume at and eavesdrop on Menaechmus E undetected. The *adulescens* is just now approaching Erotium's house, having been unexpectedly detained at the forum all day. Little does he know how much trouble he's walking into. Soliloquizing about his bad luck, he casually confesses all of his crimes:

Yes, my day of play's been wasted!
A tasty luncheon made to order,
A tastier mistress left in waiting ...
The minute I was finished
I high-tailed it right on out of the forum.
She's angry, no doubt about that,
But I'll beat that rap with the pashmina –
Yes, the one that I stole from my wife and gave to Erotium today!

597–601

Wife and parasite ambush the young man, who sputters in surprise. Menaechmus E gestures to his parasite, desperately pleading for his help. Peniculus, however, has no interest in helping this traitor. Instead, he throws his patron under the chariot and spurs on the wife's attack:

Peniculus (to Menaechmus)   Why so afraid?
Menaechmus [E]   I'm not afraid of anything!
Peniculus   There's one thing you seem all wrapped up in fear about.
   And you really shouldn't have finished off that feast without me.
   [To the wife] Keep on him!
Menaechmus [E]   Quiet, you!
Peniculus   Damn it, I'm not going to be quiet! Look, he's giving me
   signals!

Menaechmus [E]   Damn it, I never blinked, winked or even nodded at you!

Peniculus   The audacity! To deny doing what we can obviously see you doing!

Menaechmus [E]   I swear by Jupiter and all the gods, wife – if that's good enough for you – That I never nodded at him!

609–617

Peniculus continues to fan the flames of marital discord, piping up to point out whenever Menaechmus E is attempting to lie or smooth-talk his wife, much to his patron's exasperation. He adds further comic relief by interjecting at heated moments to huff about his lost lunch: 'Go right ahead and finish off a feast without me, and then grab a garland, get drunk, and mock me right here in front of the house' (628–629). His fury over his prandial snub serves as a ridiculous counterpoint to the Wife's weightier wrath over her husband's adultery and larceny.

Peniculus and the *matrona* finally wear Menaechmus E down, and the husband begrudgingly agrees to return his wife's *palla*. Ever the opportunist, Peniculus asks the *matrona* what reward she'll give him for his help. The *matrona*, who is savvier than her foolish husband, tells the parasite that she'll return the favour next time he's in a similar situation (664). Peniculus thus skulks away empty-handed and empty-stomached, an unusual outcome for a parasite. He addresses the audience in one final aside, ever self-aware of his situation. Recognizing that he has burned his bridges with both husband and wife, he declares that he will hie himself to the forum to find a new benefactor (667). A capable charlatan, he leaves the audience with the impression that he'll be just fine, especially in an ethical underworld like Epidamnus.

g) The wife

Marriage is a funny thing in Roman Comedy. On the one hand, it is held up as the end-game of romantic relationships, the happily-ever-after to which an *adulescens* and his sweetheart aspire, assuming of course that she turns out to be a socially compatible mate. On the other hand, with very few exceptions (notably, Alcumena in *Amphitruo* and the two sisters in *Stichus*), married life is routinely caricatured as rancorous, indeed downright torturous, with callous husbands set in opposition to shrewish wives. What are we supposed to make of this dissonance?

To answer that question, let us take a closer look at Menaechmus E's mate. She is drawn in such bold stereotypical strokes that Plautus doesn't even bother to give her a name. She's referred to only as *matrona* or 'wife'; her identity is entirely dependent on her relationship to her husband. She can be further classified as an *uxor dotata* or a 'dowered wife', a subcategory of comedic wives who bring their own wealth into the marriage (and don't let their husbands forget it!).

Dowries play a key role in the precarious power dynamic between spouses in Roman Comedy.[12] In ancient Rome, women could retain possession of their dowries as a kind of safety net in the event of a husband's death or divorce. Treggiari (1991: 323–4) notes the volatility of this arrangement:

> Almost everything about a Roman dowry is ambivalent. It is meant to help secure the maintenance of the wife during a marriage or it is her insurance policy in case the marriage ends. It is transferred to the husband but may be recoverable by the wife's family. It can be cash or moveable or immoveable property or a combination of all these. It may stay with the husband's family or with the wife's or their joint offspring. Husbands may see a large dowry as an attraction or a liability – and their attitudes may be different before and after the wedding.

In Roman comedies, *uxores dotatae* often hold the purse-strings with an iron fist and parlay that into control over their good-for-nothing husbands, who inevitably respond by engaging in errant behaviour. This, in turn, perpetuates a self-destructive cycle in which the wife imperiously lashes out at her husband and the husband obstinately misbehaves further. The Roman playwrights found this pattern to be a rich source of comic material.

Menaechmus E and the unnamed *matrona* are a paradigmatic example of this kind of dysfunctional marriage. Indeed, from

Menaechmus E's first entrance, he casts his wife as a villain of cartoonish proportions:

> *If you weren't so nasty, stupid, bitchy and just plain nuts,*
> *You'd pick your likes and dislikes with an eye to pleasing me – your*
>   *husband!*
> *If after today you keep treating me this way, I guarantee*
> *I'll see you're escorted straight out of this house and home to Daddy.*
> *Every time I step out of the house you're in my face with impositions and*
>   *inquisitions:*
> *'Where are you going?' 'What are you doing?' 'What business do you have?'*
> *'What are you up to?' 'What's that you've got?' 'What were you doing?'*
> *I have to declare every little thing I've done or am doing:*
> *It's like I brought a customs officer into my house, not a wife!*
> *It's clear I've spoiled you, so here's the new program:*
> *Seeing as I lavish you with personal slaves, household provisions,*
> *Wool, a wardrobe, cash, and fancy accessories, the smart thing for you to do*
> *Is to stop spying on your husband. So get with it now!*
> *And do you know what? To reward you for all your spying,*
> *I'll be having dinner out today – with my favorite whore!*
>
>   110–124

Fully committing to his misogynistic tirade, he tries to connect with the married men in the audience: 'Where are the guys who know the only marital bliss is extramarital? And how about some props for my bold defeat of that battle-axe?' (128–129). He can't help but brag about his perfidy, and in so doing, he validates his wife's suspicions. Herein lies the key to understanding their dynamic: *both* husband *and* wife are deeply – in their own ways, equally – flawed. As Duckworth (1952: 255) observes, 'many wives in Roman Comedy are presented in an unattractive light, as shrewish, hot-tempered, suspicious, extravagant. But in many cases they have faithless husbands.' Yes, she's awful, but then again, so is he. Ironically, they are quite well suited to one another.

Her reputation preceding her, we finally meet the *matrona* in person at 559, when she and Peniculus prepare to ambush Menaechmus E. Their exchange supports every stereotype that the audience has been primed to expect of her character. She is angry, she is shrill, she is out to catch her wayward husband and punish him accordingly: 'So I'm supposed to put up with the kind of marriage in which my husband steals everything there is in the house and gives it to his girlfriend?' (559–561). The audience, of course, knows that her fury is justified; Menaechmus E *is* stealing from and cheating on her. However, as Muecke (1987: 19) notes, she is so 'unpleasantly shrewish in defense of her rights ... that even though she is the injured party we are not allowed to sympathise with her in her plight'. Indeed, even the non-lyric meter reinforces the antipathy we are supposed to feel toward her. Gratwick (1982: 111) observes:

> Female characters ... are given highly operatic parts in proportion to their charms: the Bacchis sisters, Palaestra and Ampelisca (*Rudens*), Adelphasium and Anterastilis (*Poenulus*), and others such never merely speak *senarii*. When women do, e.g., the girl in *Persa*, it is because the mode has been established for the scene by an unsympathetic male character. *Matrona* in *Menaechmi* is a significant exception: she has the initiative at 559 ff. and 701ff., but she chooses senarii, a formal hint that we are not to feel too sorry for her.

She is too stern and serious a character for the comedic world in which she operates and, as a result, she is stuck being pigeonholed as a buzzkill blocking character.

Plautus takes this stock figure and pushes her to prodigious extremes. When the *matrona* asks the parasite how to deal with her husband, he replies, 'Oh I vote for your usual treatment: give him absolute hell!' (569). She goes all in, nagging and needling him incessantly until he finally cracks: 'You're full of crap ... You're full of crap ... You're full of crap ... Crap-free at last! .... You're full of crap again ...' (*nugas agis ... nugas agis ... nugas agis ... nunc tu non nugas agis ... rur<s>um nunc nugas agis*, 621–625). A force to be reckoned with, she holds all the power in this argument and so dominates her weaselly husband. As Fantham (2015: 92) notes, 'what puts wives [such as our *matrona*] in control of the action is their husbands' guilt'. Making it clear who wears the pants in their relationship, she locks him out of the house until he returns her things: 'You will [get it back] if you know what's good for you: You won't step foot in this house again unless you've got that pashmina' (661–662). With that, the *matrona* turns her back on him and storms off.

She next appears at 704, when she steps outside to check on her husband and instead discovers Menaechmus S wearing the *palla*. Much of the humour in the ensuing Mistaken Identity Bit relies on the contrast between this scene and the preceding one with Menaechmus E. Unlike his brother, Menaechmus S is *not* married to the *matrona* and is therefore neither guilty of infidelity nor subject to her authority. When she unleashes her wrath on him, Menaechmus S can – and does – rebuke her in kind:

> **Menaechmus [S]**   Woman, do you happen to know why the Greeks of old
> Called Hecuba a bitch?
> **Matrona**   I most certainly do not!
> **Menaechmus [S]**   It's because she behaved exactly as you are now.
> She kept piling curse after curse on anyone she ran into.
> Not surprisingly, she began to be known as 'the bitch.'
>
> 714–718

His insults are more than she can take. She vows to divorce him (twice!), marking the first time that a Mistaken Identity Bit has meaningfully threatened the stability of Menaechmus E's life. Losing patience with the screwball people in this screwball place, Menaechmus S tells her that he doesn't care *what* she does:

> **Matrona**   I will not put up with your outrageous conduct anymore!
> I'd sooner spend the rest of my life as a divorcee
> Than tolerate your disgusting and disgraceful deeds!
> **Menaechmus [S]**   And why should I care whether or not you tolerate your marriage
> Or if you're planning to divorce? Or is it the local custom here
> To blather on about your personal business to every stranger who comes to town?
> **Matrona**   Blather on? Why! I absolutely will not tolerate this anymore!
> I won't stand for your behavior! I'd rather be a divorcee.

Menaechmus [S]   Oh hell, for all I care you can be a divorcee
Up until the very end of Jupiter's reign.

719–728

The *matrona* thus finds herself in an impotent position; she is unable to do what she does best, namely tear her husband down. She decides to call for back-up, summoning her father to come to her defence. The old man soon appears, singing a show-stopping ditty in which he gripes about the nuisances of old age and dealing with his daughter. In an unexpected turn of events, he criticizes her for being a typical *uxor dotata*, further underlining the distinctive traits of this comedic stereotype: '*That's the way it is with women who are armed with a dowry. They're out of control. Their goal? Enslaving their husbands!*' (*ita istaec solent quae viros subservire sibi postulant, dote fretae feroces*, 766–767). The old man thus reveals that he may not be as sympathetic to the *matrona*'s predicament as she would have hoped. When she tells him about her husband's transgressions, the old man takes his son-in-law's side:

Senex   How many times have I told you to pamper your husband,
   And not monitor what he's doing, where he's going, and what he's
      up to?
Matrona   But he's having sex with the hooker living right next door!
Senex   Makes sense to me. And thanks to your surveillance, I
      guarantee you he'll be having more of it.
Matrona   And he drinks there!
Senex   Do you think he'll stop drinking there
   Or anywhere else he wants to because of you? Damn it, now you're
      way out of line!
   You might as well order him to refuse dinner invitations,
   Or not invite a guest into his own home! What do you want your
      husband to be?
   Your slave? Oh, and while you're at it, sit him down among the
      maids,
   And give him all the tools he needs to card wool.
Matrona   Well, it seems I only brought you here to plead my husband's
      case, not mine!

You're supposed to be on my side, but here you are taking his!
Senex   If he's done wrong,
I'll chew him out all right – and even more so than I did you.
But as it is, you're very well stocked with jewelry and clothes, maids,
And household supplies. How about taking a healthier attitude
about things?

787–802

Brutally unsentimental, the old man reinforces the misogynistic thread that runs throughout *Menaechmi*. As the *senex* sees it, the *matrona* has it pretty good and, accordingly, she should cut her husband some slack. Echoing his son-in-law's criticisms from the start of the play, he effectively blames her for driving Menaechmus E into Erotium's arms. It is only when the *matrona* reveals that her husband has been stealing from her that the *senex* is willing to reconsider his position: 'Hmm, bad stuff, if that's what he's doing. If not, it's your bad for accusing an innocent man' (805–806). If indeed Menaechmus E is stealing from her – from them – his crime becomes a financial matter, which supersedes a frivolous emotional one.

When the *senex* tries to get his son-in-law's side of the story, Menaechmus S feigns his fit of madness, striking terror into the hearts of the *matrona* and her father.

Matrona   Just look at the color of his eyes! He's so pale
About his forehead and temples! And his eyes are flashing!
Menaechmus [S]   That gives me an idea. Since they've already declared me insane,
Why not just go with the flow and scare them away?
Matrona   His face is all twisted and his mouth's hanging open! What should I do, father?
Senex   Come over here, daughter, as far away from him as you can get!

829–834

Menaechmus S intensifies his threats, legitimately frightening the *matrona* and sending her fleeing for her life. After all she's endured, she makes one last appeal for the audience's sympathy: 'For a woman to have to hear such things!' (*sumne ego mulier misera quae illaec audio?*, 852). Her final words here humanize her for one brief moment, adding a hint of depth to an otherwise one-dimensional character. This is the last we see of her, though her presence prevails right up until the penultimate line of the play when Messenio announces:

> Announcing an auction at Menaechmus' a week from today!
> Everything must go: slaves, furniture, house, country estate.
> Each and every thing goes to the highest bidder, all sales cash only!
> Even his wife's on the block, if any blockhead wants her!
> I doubt she'll account for more than a penny's worth of the proceeds.
> As for right now, spectators: give us a loud round of applause. And
> good luck to you all!

1157–1162

In this way, the wife bookends the comedy from offstage; the main action of the play essentially opens with Menaechmus E thundering angrily at his wife and ends with him planning to auction her off. She is, in many ways, the comic catalyst in *Menaechmi*. Her dysfunctional dynamic with her husband plays a key role in motivating every (bad) decision he makes, and it reverberates through his interactions with just about every other character. She is such a dominant force in the story that she even shapes its resolution. The happy ending derives not only from the brothers' reunion with one another and Messenio's emancipation, but also Menaechmus E's liberation from his wife.

To return to our earlier question, then, what are we supposed to make of this travesty of marriage in general and wives in particular? Many scholars simply dismiss the misogyny as a trope. As Muecke (1987: 19) suggests, 'this is exploitation of a comic stereotype and not to be taken seriously as social commentary'. Duckworth (1952: 284) observes that 'there is little in married happiness that lends itself to comic treatment; thus the delineation of older husbands and wives departs from real life and becomes a conventional means of arousing laughter; much that we find on marriage is not to be taken seriously'. For sure, this caricature of marriage is a comic shtick and one that has endured the test of time, from Greek Middle and New Comedy to

contemporary stand-up ('take my wife .... please!'). We can't (ahem)
divorce it entirely from social commentary, however. Its serious
undercurrent is what gives the stereotype its satirical bite. It illustrates
Roman Comedy's unique ability to shine a light on some of the darker
aspects of Roman culture, including slavery and misogyny, from a
privileged place of ludic licence. In so doing, it invites theatregoers to sit
with, think about, and perhaps even find some humour and/or humanity
in these uncomfortable issues.

h) The old man

By and large, the *senex* is as conventional a stock character as they come.
He is a doddering old fogey, whose toothless tirades and geriatric body
language naturally lend themselves to virtuosic voiced and physical
comedy. Like his daughter, his role is so one-dimensional that Plautus
once again eschews naming him and simply refers to him by his type:
senex ('old man'). This figure appears in all but three of Plautus' extant
plays (i.e. *Amphitruo, Curculio, Persa*). In just about every other Plautine
comedy, at least one *senex* is directly involved in the main plot; four of
them putter around the stage in *Trinummus*. His role in *Menaechmi* –
and, for that matter, *Truculentus* – is relatively ancillary to the action. At
the same time, even as minor characters, *senes* tend to steal the scenes
in which they appear.

The *senex* typically plays one of four roles in Roman Comedy: parent,
aged would-be lover, helpful friend or miser. As a parent, he ranges
from an overindulgent to an overly strict guardian; as an aged lover, he
is often a buffoonish adulterer and/or a rival with an *adulescens* over the
affections of a girl; as a helpful friend, he may be a kindly neighbour,
who fondly remembers the pleasures of his own youth and intervenes
in whatever scheme is afoot to support the young lovers; as a miser, he
jealously hoards his money and/or his daughter. These roles are not
mutually exclusive; they sometimes overlap with one another.

Once again, Plautus reimagines this stock character to suit the
comedic needs of *Menaechmi*. As Muecke (1987: 19) observes, 'the role

in which the father appears is not typical'. She notes that his closest analogue is Smikrines, the father of the young wife in Menander's (fragmentary) *Epitrepontes*. Like our *senex*, Smikrines gets drawn in to the plot when he discovers that his son-in-law has walked out on his wife (i.e. Smikrines' daughter) and is frittering away his finances on prostitutes and parties. Similar to the old man in *Menaechmi*, his umbrage is mainly motivated by the threat that his son-in-law's behaviour poses to his daughter's dowry. In this way, both *senes* generally fall under the broad categories of 'parent' and 'miser'. Whatever *persona* the *senex* adopts – parent, aged lover, helpful friend, miser – his most consistent traits are his (old) age and (male) sex. As Duckworth (1952: 243) notes:

> The all-inclusive term 'old man' is very misleading. Other characters – professional roles such as the banker or slavedealer – may be as advanced in years but they are not listed as *senes*. Actually, the *senex* as a role refers merely to the older male members of the various households; as opposed to the *adulescentes* who are usually in their late teens or early twenties (cf. *Bacch.* 422), the *senes* are men somewhat past middle age, presumably in their fifties or early sixties . . . few seem as aged and decrepit as the father-in-law of Menaechmus [E] who complains that his strength has deserted him: his body is a burden and he can no longer move nimbly
>
> *Men.* 756 ff.

In our play, Plautus inflates and explodes this stereotype. This *senex* is not just an elderly paternal figure; he is Old Age and 'old school' misogyny incarnate. He explicitly acknowledges as much, when he first hobbles onto the stage:

> *As my old age allows and need be,*
> *I'll plant a foot forward and plod forth as fast as I can.*
> *It isn't easy for me – make no mistake about it.*
> *I've lost my nimbleness long, long ago.*
> *Old age's buried me, I've got a burden for a body, my strength's a distant memory.*
> *The rougher old age is, the rawer the deal for a sickly person:*

It brings in its wake a mountain of miseries.
I could name every last one of them, but that'd take too long.
The thing that's weighing heaviest on my mind right now
Is what trouble there could possibly be
To make my daughter send for me so suddenly.
I've not a clue of what it is she wants
Or why she's summoned me.
Still, I can pretty well guess what's up:
Some dispute with her husband's arisen

753–765

As Gratwick (1993: 208) observes, the substance of the *senex's* song can be broken into four sections, each with its own metrical character:

(a) (753–60) 'O the ills of old age, so slowing me!'; (b) (761–3) 'What can my daughter want?'; (c) (764–71) 'It's a domestic quarrel I suppose: I wonder who's to blame?"; (d) 'There they are: it's as I thought.' Each section has its own metrical character: (a) A slow bacchiac 'para-system' [with its] occasional dragged feet $(\ldots --- /, \ldots \smile \smile --$ for $\ldots \smile --)$ are expressive of Senex's slow gait.

The meter, then, combines with the words to underscore and exaggerate the old man's senescence.

The *senex's* extreme old age colours his extreme views about women and marriage. When he first tells his daughter that she should obey her husband, rather than spy on him, and he enthusiastically defends his son-in-law's rebellious drinking and whoring, the audience is likely to be as surprised as the *matrona*. At the same time, his words contribute to his emerging caricature as a radically conservative old coot. There is virulent misogyny here, for sure, and yet it's ultimately undercut by the absurdity of the figure voicing it. At no point does Plautus encourage his audience to identify with or heroize the *senex*. On the contrary, the playwright renders him such a clown that he enfeebles the old man's pronouncements as well as his physique.

His frailty, ironically, becomes a kind of 'running' gag. Plautus plays up the incongruity between the *senex's* infirmity and the physical situations in which he finds himself, for example, his utter defenselessness in the 'mad' scene when Menaechmus S threatens to 'pulverize his bones, limbs and joints with the stick he carries', 'grab a double-edged axe and slice off this old man's guts right down to the bone', and 'take a span of horses, untamed, vicious. Mount [his] chariot and pave the path beneath [him] with this elderly, toothless, and smelly lion' (855–864). One can imagine the dynamic dramaturgical possibilities of contrasting the body language of the frail *senex* with that of the menacing *adulescens*. The playwright exploits the old man's physicality once again at 881, when he brings the *senex* back onstage after a mere five-line hiatus, during which time the old man claims to have gone off in search of the doctor, waited at length for him, and walked all the way back to Menaechmus E's house. He even complains that he strained both his hindquarters and his eyes from sitting and keeping watch for so long (882–883). What is more, the old man criticizes the *doctor* for moving so slowly: 'Look at how he walks! Can you get it out of ant-gear?' (888). This joke picks up on the conceit first introduced by the Prologue back at 49 (*Nunc in Epidamnum pedibus redeundum est mihi*); one really can travel instantaneously in Epidamnus! The impossible speed demanded by this bit further underlines the old man's old age and undermines the realism of his comic world. Our *senex's* defining characteristic, then, is his preternatural dotage, manifest in his old-timer body language and old-timey chauvinism. Plautus takes every opportunity to milk this for laughs by setting him in opposition to his daughter, to younger more virile characters, and to the laws of physics.

i) The doctor

Rounding out the cast of *Menaechmi* is the *medicus* ('doctor'). Like the *matrona* and the *senex*, he is also unnamed. As Gratwick (1993: 221) observes, his anonymity is less striking than theirs because he is a professional type, and Plautus seems not to have had a consistent policy about either naming or not naming such figures (e.g. a cook, a parasite, a soldier). Our doctor is unique, however, in that he is the only example of this professional type in all of extant Roman Comedy. Plautus may have written another play by the name of *Parasitus Medicus* ('Parasite Doctor', a surefire hit), though the script has been lost. Our only attestation for it is the attribution of three fragments. He mentions doctors elsewhere in his corpus, primarily as punch lines, for example at *Mercator* 472–473, when a character declares that he will go to the doctor in order to kill himself, and at *Rudens* 1304–1306, when a character makes a play on the words *medicus* ('doctor') and *mendicus* ('beggar'). The *medicus* of *Menaechmi*, then, is quite literally one of a kind. He is not just a comic doctor, he is the comic doctor.

To develop this character, Plautus drew on prevailing public opinions about medical practices and practitioners. Doctors had long been contentious figures in the Roman world.[13] Pliny records that the first doctor to come to Rome was a Greek man named Archagathus in 219 BCE (*Natural History* 29.12-13). From that point on and well into the first century CE, the medical profession in Rome was inextricably associated with Greek culture and, as von Staden (1996: 369) observes, this caused a great deal of anxiety for the Romans:

> From the first attested arrival of a Greek physician in Rome, the host culture's response to Greek medicine was marked both by enthusiastic reception and by abusive rejection, both by generous embrace and by fearful hostility. This profound ambivalence had its roots, *inter alia,* in differences, both real and imagined, between the institutional, professional, familial, literary, and socio-linguistic cultures of Rome and Greece.

This xenophobia, coupled with the zeal for proto-science and pseudoscience of Plautus' day, was a goldmine of material for the comedic playwrights.

In addition to contemporary Roman attitudes toward doctors, Plautus also drew inspiration from stereotypes handed down from the Greek New Comic tradition. Despite the dearth of evidence, it seems that the doctor was a particularly popular figure in Greek New Comedy; Antiphanes, Aristophon, Philemon and Theophilus all wrote plays entitled *The Doctor* ('Ιατρός).[14] The best surviving analogue is the parody of a doctor in Menander's *Aspis* (433–464). Here the figure is a co-conspirator in the clever slave's plan to fake an ally's death in order to trick a blocking character. They realize an imposter will suit their needs just as well: 'Know any foreign doctor who's a joker, a bit bogus?' 'No, by Zeus, I don't!' 'Well, you should.' 'Here's a thought. I'll come back with one of my friends. I'll borrow toupée, cloak, and stick for him. He'll speak a foreign dialect all he can' (ξενικόν τιν' οἶσθ' ἰατρόν, Χαιρέα, ἀστεῖον, ὑπαλαζόνα; μὰ τὸν Δί, οὐ πάνυ. καὶ μὴν ἔδει. τί δὲ τοῦτο; τῶν ἐμῶν τινα ἥξω συνηθῶν παραλαβὼν καὶ προκόμιον αἰτήσομαι καὶ χλανίδα καὶ βακτηρίαν αὐτῷ, ξενιεῖ δ' ὅσ' ἂν δύνηται, 374–379; translation Arnott [1979: 62–3]). The fake doctor arrives at 433 donning a stereotypical disguise and adopting a stereotypical dialect. Spouting nonsensical medical jargon in a heavy accent, he clumsily 'examines' the patient and immediately pronounces that has fallen fatally ill.

It seems likely that the doctors of Greek New Comedy regularly spoke in a distinctive Doric dialect; this would have been one of the hallmarks of the comedic stereotype in Athenian performance. As Lloyd-Jones (1971: 187) notes, this theory is supported by a fragment from Alexis' comedy, *The Woman Who Took Mandragora*, in which 'someone says that if a native doctor recommends giving a patient beetroot, calling that vegetable by its Attic name of τευτλίον, he is despised, but if a foreigner prescribes it, pronouncing it σεῦτλον, people treat him with respect'. Gratwick (1993: 221–2) proposes the following explanation:

> The school of Hippocrates belonged to Doric-speaking Cos and a good deal of the pseudo-Hippocratic corpus is in that dialect. This is like the stage convention by which doctors in English comedy and novels used to have Scottish names and accents because of the pre-eminence of the Edinburgh school of medicine in the nineteenth century. It is likely enough that the author of *Menaechmi* had followed this convention in presenting his 'Dr Cameron'; but since Pl. could not match the medical connotations of the Doric dialect in Latin, he has sacrificed that facet of the presentation, confidently relying on the substance of the role for comic effect.

Unable to capture in Latin the aural humour of the Greek, Plautus leans into the doctor's other stock trait: his penchant for grim and graphic diagnoses. In his translation of Menander's *Aspis*, Arnott (1979: 76–7) attempts to capture the melodrama and 'foreignness' of the 'doctor's' speech with a Scottish dialect: 'He willna live at a', I say. He's vomitin' bile. [The affliction] dims [his sight], [...] and for (?) his een [...] he aften faims at the mooth, an' [...] his look's funereal' (οὐ πάμπαν οὗτός ἐστί τοι βιώσιμος.ἀνερεύγεταί τι τᾶς χολᾶς· ἐπισκοτεῖ]εντ .[..] καὶ τοῖς ὄμμασιπ]υκνὸν ἀναφρίζει τε καὶ] .ας ἐκφορὰν βλέπει, 450–454). On the one hand, the imposter happily hams it up, implausibly over-acting the role as far as the audience is concerned. On the other hand, his performance succeeds in tricking the blocking character, who leaves convinced that the patient is not long for this world. His cameo is brief, but memorable., Like we saw with the figure of the *ancilla*, the doctor in *Aspis* is effectively a showpiece for this stock character to perform his stock shtick.

In *Menaechmi*, the doctor is similarly something of a quack with a penchant for catastrophizing. Before even laying eyes on his patient, he leaps to some colourful conclusions about him: 'Now, what's that you say he has? Out with it, old man! Case of Goblinitis? Ceresmania? Give me the scoop. Does he have a history of narcolepsy? Angioedema?' (889–891). The doctor calls his own competence into question, when he tells the old man, 'No need to worry: I'll sigh deeply at his bedside six-hundred times a day. That's proof that I'm concerned he gets the best possible care' (896–897).

The doctor seems to have at least some working knowledge of ancient medical practices.[15] At 913, he refers to hellebore, a poisonous plant which was used to treat insanity, and at 915 he inquires whether Menaechmus E drinks white or red wine, presumably invoking the medicinal properties of these. According to Cato, *Agr.*, 115, dark wine was thought to be a laxative, and white wine an astringent. The doctor peppers his patient with questions as he tries to gather his medical history:

> **Medicus**   Tell me, do your eyes ever become crustaceous?
> **Menaechmus [E]**   You scumbag! What do you think I am, a lobster?
> **Medicus**   Tell me this: have you ever noticed your intestines rumbling?

Menaechmus [E]   When I'm full, there's no rumbling. There's lots of
rumbling when I'm empty.

Medicus   Geeze, that doesn't sound like crazy talk to me!
Do you sleep straight through the night? Do you fall asleep right
away?

Menaechmus [E]   I sleep perfectly, if all my bills are paid.
May Jupiter and all the gods blast you, Mr. Inquisitor!

Medicus   Now he's starting to rave. Judging by what he says, you'd
better watch out.

923–931

Provoking Menaechmus E to his breaking point, the doctor eventually
– erroneously – becomes convinced that the young man is indeed mad.
He tells the angry *adulescens*, 'I'll have you on liquid hellebore for
twenty days or so', to which Menaechmus E replies, 'I'll hang you up and
poke you with spikes for thirty days' (950–951). With that, the doctor
leaves to prepare for his patient's arrival at his home. Like the fake
doctor in Menander's *Aspis*, then, our doctor's sole purpose in the play
is to contribute a comedic cameo in which he performs all of his greatest
hits (grandiloquent technical jibber-jabber, dire prognoses,
overconfident and inaccurate quackery), fulfilling his function as a
figure of fun.

*

In *Menaechmi*, Plautus operates within the key conventions of his genre:
he sets the play in a typical Graeco-Roman hybrid world, he populates
it with familiar stock character types, and he has them interact with one
another in familiar stock situations. In this way, the playwright fulfils
the audience's expectations of what a Roman Comedy should look,
sound and feel like. At the same time, he breathes new life into both the
setting and the *dramatis personae*, exploiting and exploding their salient
attributes in order to fit the narrative goals of – and optimize the
humour in – this particular play. With metatheatrical winks to the
audience, Plautus calls attention to these time-honoured conventions
and also demonstrates their plasticity.

TWINterplay of Comic Language and Stage Business: Bits, Banter and Buffoonery

Humour is a tricky subject to write about. In a way, doing so can defeat the purpose. The truth is, jokes often become less funny the more we try to explain them. Parsing out the technical elements of a comic bit might allow us to appreciate the skill and creativity that went into it, but it also divests the joke of its ability to surprise us. Humour very often hinges on The Unexpected, whether it disrupts an established pattern (a-b-a-b-a-b-MONKEY!) or breaks a rule about how the world works. This is why a well-turned one-liner or a well-timed pie in the face will always be a reliable source of laughter. Humour is most electric in the moment and strives towards a sense of spontaneity, no matter how many rewrites, rehearsals or reruns are part of the process. The dynamic, unpredictable, 'live' experience of comedy inevitably loses something in the translation from execution to explication.

Furthermore, trying to explain why a joke is funny is like trying to describe why a song lifts your spirits or a painting moves you to tears. One could analyse the patterns of notes, rhythms, contours or colours, but the fact is art is fundamentally subjective and deeply personal. The success of a joke depends as much on the audience's circumstances and their willingness to play along as it does on the comedian's craftsmanship. As noted in previous chapters, Messenio's song-and-dance about his fear of being tortured (966–989) would have landed very differently with the slaves, freed-people and free people in the audience, and further still among individuals within those categories. The best that a writer of popular comedy, ancient or modern, can do is design jokes that work on multiple levels simultaneously or speak to different audiences at any given time. The best that a scholar of popular comedy can do is to point to the polyphony of perspectives, offer basic socio-historical context, and acknowledge the impossibility of speculating broadly and accurately about audience reception.

And yet Plautine humour demands to be analysed. It is inherently, explicitly, unapologetically *formulaic* and, as such, it relies heavily on the audience's familiarity with – and indulgence of – its conventions. Yes, the play stands on its own as a fun and frothy caper requiring no prior knowledge or real-time effort to enjoy, but it rewards an informed, sympathetic audience on a whole other level. Anyone who had heard about or attended a Roman comedy before would have known exactly what to expect when they sat down in that theatre, from the cast of characters, to the broad strokes of the plot, and of course the happy ending. They came to see what Plautus would do with them *this* time, how he could spin the story anew with fresh and lyrical language and exciting, farcical stage action.

Herein lies the key to Plautine humour: it is the playwright's ability to embrace the predictable and produce The Unexpected. Plautus leans into the audience's preconceived notions about Roman Comedy, and strategically satisfies or subverts their expectations in order to keep them on their toes. *Menaechmi* is a masterpiece of this style of humour. The plot is as predictable as they come; the brothers' reunion is largely a foregone conclusion from early on in the prologue (arguably from the title itself) and the verbal and visual jokes are all typical Plautine fare, as we will see shortly. The comedian gives the audience exactly what they came for: a gimmicky set-up, stylized metatheatre, punchy word play, clownish physical comedy. His genius lies in the way he shrewdly modulates the tempo and zigs instead of zags in order to optimize the dramatic tension and the element of surprise.

With these considerations in mind, then, let us take a closer look at some of the hallmarks of Plautine humour that appear in our play so that we can get a better sense of what makes his style both distinctive and funny. This chapter will begin by examining the Mistaken Identity Bit, the mainspring of the plot and much of its comedy. From there, it will investigate Plautus' use of metatheatrical devices to bend, flex and stretch the boundaries of dramatic illusion. After that, it will focus on the sights and sounds that epitomize and energize his staging and dialogue. Finally, it will unpack the play's 'happy' ending in all its technical and conceptual absurdity. By familiarizing ourselves with the Plautine playbook, we can better understand how the playwright both panders to and cuts against audience expectation and, in so doing, how he makes *Menaechmi* his own.

The Mistaken Identity Bit

Plautus did not invent the Mistaken Identity Bit, but he did play an important role in its time-honoured tradition. His work is a vital link in the chain connecting its appearance in Greek Middle and New Comedy to Renaissance and early modern drama. The mistaken identicals motif was a popular feature of Greek Middle and New Comedy.[1] Menander's *Dis Exapatōn* offers the most prominent extant example: among other plot twists and turns, a misunderstanding over the identities of two sisters who share the same name (Bacchis of Athens and Bacchis of Samos) threatens the friendship of the young men who love them. In addition, Damen (1989: 410–11) identifies at least eleven Greek and two non-Plautine Roman plays that reference doubles in their titles: '*Didumoi*: Alexis, Anaxandrides, Antiphanes, Euphron, Xenarchus; *Didumai*: Antiphanes, Aristophon, Menander; *Homoioi/Homoiai*: Antiphanes, Ephippus, Posidippus. Alexis (or Antidotos) wrote a *Homoia* which may also include a mistaken identical ... [Among the Romans], Novius wrote a *Gemini* and Laberius a *Gemelli*.' This list likely represents only a fraction of the Middle and New Comic plays that utilized the twin trope in one form or another. There were undoubtedly many others, whose titles simply don't spotlight it.

Plautus himself employed variations on the Mistaken Identity Bit in four extant plays – *Amphitruo, Bacchides, Menaechmi* and *Miles Gloriosus* – and in at least two lost ones, *Lenones Gemini (Twin Pimps)*

and *Trigemini (Triplets)*. In each of the extant comedies, he experiments
with the motif, sometimes making it central to the plot, other times
featuring it as an auxiliary bit; sometimes casting one actor to play both
'twins', other times requiring a minimum of two; sometimes calling for
the twins to visually resemble one another, other times only calling
them by the same name. In *Bacchides*, for example, Plautus' adaptation
of Menander's *Dis Exapatōn*, the comic confusion is based primarily on
the fact that both sisters are *named* Bacchis. Beyond one dubious
fragment, which may or may not belong to the play (*sicut lacte lactis
similest*, fr. V; cf. *Menaechmi* 1088–1090 *nec lacte est lacti<s> . . . similius
quam hic tui est,* both quotes suggesting that the doubles are 'as similar
as one drop of milk to another') there is nothing in the existing dialogue
or larger plot that requires them to look like one another. Further, as
Damen (1989: 419) notes, they appear onstage together twice and must
have been played by two different actors, since they speak to each other
in their first shared scene. It is impossible to know how closely the
production chose to emphasize their resemblance. The Bacchis sisters
may have been twins in name only.

In *Miles Gloriosus*, on the other hand, the 'twins'' similitude is the
heart and soul of the shtick. In one brief but memorable episode, a
young girl (Philocomasium) pretends to be her own double so as to
deceive a slave (Sceledrus) who caught her secretly cavorting with her
lover. In order for the sting to succeed, the 'twins' must appear absolutely
identical; Philocomasium must convince Sceledrus that he can't believe
his own eyes. She quickly passes back and forth through a hole
connecting neighbouring houses to support the illusion that she is two
different people. What makes this silly set-up soar is the fact that both
twins are conspicuously played not just by the same actor, but by the
same character. A big part of the fun is watching Philocomasium rise to
the dramaturgical challenge of nimbly alternating between houses and
roles. The audience, smug in their superior understanding of the
situation, also enjoys watching Sceledrus muddle through his confusion.
Luckily for Philocomasium, at no point does Sceledrus demand to see
both sisters together at the same time.

Amphitruo, Plautus' other great mistaken identicals comedy, is arguably the closest surviving analogue to *Menaechmi*. As in our play, the plot and comedic engine of *Amphitruo* revolve around twins being confused with one another. Plautus ups the ante here by featuring not one, but *two* sets of identicals: a mortal master–slave pair and an immortal master–slave pair. The gods Jupiter and Mercury disguise themselves as the humans Amphitruo and his slave Sosia, respectively, so that the king of the gods can deceive and seduce Amphitruo's wife. Like in *Bacchides*, multiple actors were needed to play these doubles since they share several speaking scenes with one another. The dialogue strongly suggests that the two pairs were identical in appearance (though very different in personalities), a bit of stage magic easily accomplished by the strategic use of masks and costumes. In the prologue, for example, Mercury announces that the gods have taken on the form of their human counterparts and that the audience will be able to distinguish him by a feather atop his hat and Jupiter by a gold tassel hanging from his (*Amph.* 140–147). If they really were mirror images of one another, this would substantiate Sosia's existential crisis when he comes face-to-face with his divine doppelgänger later on in the play.

Plautus draws on many of these conventional, 'predictable' features of the Mistaken Identity Bit in *Menaechmi*: as in *Bacchides*, the brothers' shared name is a fertile source of comic confusion; as in *Miles Gloriosus*, the playwright exploits the exciting metatheatrical possibilities of having one actor play both twins (right up to the final recognition scene); as in *Amphitruo*, the story centres on the misapprehension of the twins and, for that matter, the theme of adultery. With *Menaechmi*, Plautus carefully selects and brings into balance the most salient and successful aspects of the motif in order to produce the ultimate mistaken identicals comedy.

Clearly Plautus – and his audience – were fans of the Mistaken Identity Bit. But what made it so funny? With a nod to all of the aforementioned obstacles to faithfully answering this question, I offer three possible explanations: (1) dramatic irony, (2) visual appeal, and (3) stagecraft. Dramatic irony – when an audience understands something that the characters do not – is the driving force behind the Mistaken Identity Bit. As complicated as the ensuing hullaballoo can become, the basic premise is about as simple as it gets: characters are confused with one another and that confusion leads to some sort of conflict. It is easy enough for the audience to grasp in the moment and easy enough for the playwright to resolve at the appropriate time. All it takes is for one character to put the glaringly obvious pieces together. Indeed, the more obvious the solution is, the more ridiculous it becomes when the characters can't see it. For example, when they first meet, Erotium will go so far as to correctly identify Menaechmus S's father and birthplace but he *still* won't be able to connect the dots (407–408). His obtuseness is all the more stunning since the whole point of his being in Epidamnus in the first place is to track down clues about his lost brother. The bit only gets funnier as the characters become more and more blinded by their confusion and further and further entangled in the consequent conflicts. The audience, on the other hand, is never in any real doubt about the inevitability of a happy ending (in one form or another) and therefore they can sit back, relax and enjoy watching the characters bumble their way through a puzzle they've already solved.

Visual appeal is another reason why the Mistaken Identity Bit is funny. Simply put, doubles are interesting to look at on a stage. Seeing identical people or objects side-by-side or in quick sequence with one another invites contrast and comparison, and it opens up exciting dramaturgical possibilities. A production could lean into the twins' resemblance (a mirror-pantomime routine is a classic example of this), or it could push against the optical echoes by giving the twins strikingly *dissimilar* body language. If one actor did play both Menaechmi, what a fun challenge it could be for him to quickly adapt his physicality according to whichever twin he was playing in the moment. It is possible that the music that accompanied Menaechmus E's entrances and abruptly stopped with those of Menaechmus S signalled something about the way they moved in addition to their personalities. On another level, scholars such as Segal (1968) and Leach (1969) also point to the psychological implications of the premise. By juxtaposing the twins' visual resemblance with their individuality, the playwright destabilizes and interrogates the very notions of self and identity. Indeed, Menaechmus S, though called 'Sosicles' as a child, even absorbs his brother's name. This exploration of ego and alter ego would have been all the more poignant if both twins were played by the same actor.

This brings us to our third point: stagecraft. The audience knows that they are in for a mistaken identicals story, but the question remains: How will the production pull off the doubling this time? Will the twins be truly identical? How will the audience tell them apart? Will they be played by one actor or two? If one, then how will the quick-change entrances and exits work? Will they confront each other face-to-face and, if so, *how*? And when? It is impossible to say how realistically any one production answered these questions, but we can see the comic potential in each choice. I would argue that the more the production leans into the absurdity of the situation, the funnier it becomes. This is especially true of plays like *Menaechmi*, where one actor can play both twins (see chapter 1). A vital part of the humour here rests on the production's ability to underline and then undermine the illusion that there are two of them. For example, at line 700, Menaechmus E exits toward one side of the stage and moments later Menaechmus S reappears from the opposite wing, mid-conversation with Messenio. This offers the star actor a unique opportunity to shine. The audience can well imagine the aerobic demands of his backstage sprint; the actor can milk this for laughs whether he chooses to playfully pause and acknowledge the metatheatre with a breathless pant or he doubles down on the illusion despite its obvious implausibility.

Plautus pulls out all the stops with the Mistaken Identity Bit in *Menaechmi*. As early as the prologue, he anticipates misunderstandings over the twins' shared name and invites the audience to be on the lookout for dramatic irony: 'Just so there's no confusion later, I repeat: BOTH BROTHERS HAVE THE SAME NAME' (47–48). He then spends the first act establishing clear-cut relationships between Menaechmus E and the satellite figures in his orbit (Peniculus, Matrona,

Erotium, Cylindrus), so that by the time Menaechmus S enters at line 226, the twin cannot help but stumble into a minefield of misapprehension. The brothers' visual resemblance further contributes to the comedic chaos, complemented by a series of talismans (the *palla*, bracelet and garland) that help the audience tell them apart while amplifying the confusion among the characters. And while we can't definitively reconstruct the nuances of the original stagecraft, we can be sure that Plautus took advantage of the dramaturgical tools at his disposal (doubling of roles, masks, costumes, props, music and movement) in order to get a laugh.

Metatheatrical devices

Metatheatre is another distinctive feature of Plautine humour.[2] The term 'metatheatre' generally refers to the ways in which a play recognizes its status as a play, that is, the ways in which it demonstrates awareness of and draws attention to its own theatrical conventions. Plautus regularly employs a recurring set of metatheatrical devices across his corpus that includes: prologues and epilogues, monologues or soliloquies, asides, role-playing and eavesdropping scenes, among others. They go a long way towards shaping the tone of his comedies, conveying the effect of the playwright sharing conspiratorial winks with his audience. Here in *Menaechmi*, Plautus uses these metatheatrical devices to cultivate the audience's connection to the play, highlight points of contact between the on- and offstage worlds, and satirize the comedic genre itself.

a) Prologue and epilogue

In the last chapter, we explored the ways in which the (capital P) Prologue calls attention to the process of performance by simultaneously acknowledging and activating its conceits. In this way, he embodies metatheatre itself. The whole purpose of his being there is to establish rapport between the world of performance and the world of the audience from the start, so that there is no sense of a division or 'fourth wall'. The Prologue will also provide technical, as well as narrative, information to the audience members about the play they are about to see. He pulls back the proverbial curtain and points out the many cracks in the theatrical façade, matter-of-factly mentioning playwrights (*poetae*, 7), comedies (*comoediis*, 7), the stereotypical Graeco-Roman 'Nowhere' setting (*nusquam*, 10), the kinds of stock characters one might expect to encounter there: a pimp, a young man, an old man, a pauper, a beggar, a parasite, a soothsayer (*modo leno, modo adulescens, modo senex, pauper, mendicus, rex, parasitus, hariolus*, 75–76) and, oh yes, this very play itself being performed (*haec agitur fabula*, 72). His blunt, procedural, unromanticized view of Roman Comedy both satirizes and substantiates the genre. He is effectively saying: 'Look, *I* know what's going on here, *you* know what's going on here, but let's just go along with it anyway, shall we?' (i.e. 'I ask that you receive it with kind ears,' *quaeso ut benignis accipiatis auribus*, 4). What begins as the verbal equivalent of an eye-roll, becomes a playful agreement to embrace the clichés in all their absurdity and try to have a good time. As a result, actors and audience become partners, actively and equally participating in the shared theatrical experience.

Menaechmi also features an epilogue, a brief speech at the end of the play which signals its conclusion. Plautine epilogues are often no longer than a few lines, sometimes offering a moral of some sort and generally closing with a valediction and solicitation for applause. Messenio delivers the epilogue in our play:

> Announcing an auction at Menaechmus' a week from today!
> Everything must go: slaves, furniture, house, country estate.
> Each and everything goes to the highest bidder, all sales cash only!
> Even his wife's on the block, if any blockhead wants her!
> I doubt she'll account for more than a penny's worth of the proceeds.
> As for right now, spectators: give us a loud round of applause. And
>   good luck to you all!
>
> 1156–1162

At first glance, this epilogue might seem like a bit of a *non sequitur* (with a final punchline at the wife's expense thrown in for good measure). In fact, it does a great deal of metatheatrical work here. While the final line is explicitly directed to the audience, the addressees of the preceding lines are more ambiguous. Is Messenio speaking to the characters in Epidamnus, the spectators in Rome, or some combination of the two? He casually erases the line demarcating on- and offstage worlds just as he 'brings the curtain down', so to speak. In so doing, he first blurs and then reinforces the dramatic boundaries of the play, drawing the audience closer just before releasing them back into their real lives and their own stories.[3] In this way, the playwright invites the audience to carry the ideas of the play home with them.

The epilogue also sums up the play's attitude toward women and slaves. Though we haven't seen the wife for a while now, the last lines conjure her memory and revive the misogyny against her. By taking one last parting shot at her, Plautus confirms the wife's role as the *real* villain in the story, not Menaechmus E with all his dubious, dissolute behaviour. She is the main blocking character, the cold bucket of water who rudely rouses our protagonist from his reverie. She is anathema to the comedic world and so the frequent butt of its jokes. As for slaves, it is no accident that Messenio gets the final word. This is one of the many ways that Plautus empowers the clever slave, a heroic figure in Roman Comedy. Messenio has just demonstrated his superior intellect by solving the mistaken identity mix-up, earning his freedom in the process. Now, he gets to neatly wrap everything up, and bask in the applause.

b) Monologue / soliloquy

The monologue, or soliloquy, is another powerful tool in Plautus' comedic kit. Slater (1985: 12) defines it as 'any speech delivered by a character who is alone or believes himself to be alone onstage. It may be addressed to the audience, self, or the gods.' The monologue in Roman Comedy can be lengthy or brief, spoken or sung. Like all metatheatrical devices, it tests the limits of the 'fourth wall', sometimes leaning up against it, other times shattering it altogether. These soliloquies serve a number of key interrelated functions: (1) they grant the audience privileged access to a character's inner thoughts, (2) they confirm the Truth as each character sees it, and (3) they strengthen the alliance between characters and audience.

Following the prologue (a distinctive monologue in its own right), we are greeted by Peniculus, who delivers his famous soliloquy on parasitism (77–109). His keen and candid self-awareness and unapologetic shamelessness immediately disarm us. He demonstrates that, although he is a talented liar when the situation demands it, he is also more than capable of telling the truth about himself and his motives. By privileging the audience with this information, he earns our trust and forges an important bond with us. He shares another monologue with the audience right around the midpoint of the play (446–465), when he laments his separation from Menaechmus E in the forum and first mistakes Menaechmus S for his brother. Peniculus's monologue quickly shifts into a series of asides (469–472, 478–479, 486, 511), inviting us to see the situation through his eyes and share in – or at least appreciate – his indignation at Menaechmus E.

Menaechmus E delivers the most monologues of all the *dramatis personae*. His first, which coincides with his grand entrance, paints a portrait of our protagonist as both a henpecked husband and a lying, thieving, verbally abusive adulterer (110–134). In fact, the first fifteen lines of his soliloquy are sung to (shouted at!) his wife, who is still inside the house. Unaware of Peniculus's presence, Menaechmus E seems to believe that he is alone onstage, which begs the question: would he have said all of these horrible things to his wife's face? I would argue that the monologue offers him a unique metatheatrical interstitial space in which he can vent more freely and broadly, partly to his wife, partly to himself, partly to the audience. The final eight lines of his monologue are fully directed to the audience, explicitly attempting to connect with us and bond over what Menaechmus E presumes are our shared values, 'Where are the guys who know the only marital bliss is extramarital?' (128).

He soliloquizes again at 571–601 (on the tedious demands of the patron–client relationship), at 668–674 (on his smug solution to his wife's eviction: seeking sanctuary in his mistress's house), at 899–908 (on how bad and confusing his day has been, particularly in his dealings with Peniculus and Erotium), at 957–965 (on the precarious state of his sanity), and at 1039–1049 (on his peculiar good luck encountering Messenio ... and his wallet!). Similar to his brother, Menaechmus S delivers his own monologue in which he contemplates (though not too deeply) the strangeness of his situation. At 548–558, he muses on his good fortune (i.e. the prostitute, cloak and bracelet that literally and figuratively fell into his lap), but he stops short of actually probing into possible explanations. Each of these metatheatrical speeches draw us into the characters' inner worlds and temporarily shift our perspective of the action to their own.

Erotium, Cylindrus, the Senex and Messenio each have a solo moment in the 'spotlight', in which they broadcast some salient information about themselves and effectively self-identify as their conventional character types. At 351–360, Erotium explicitly confesses her economic motives to the audience before pouncing on an unsuspecting Menaechmus S: 'Oh, he's over there: My finest and foremost source of income! As long as his cash keeps pouring in, he reigns supreme in this house!' (357–359). Likewise, at 273–277, Cylindrus informs us that he's back from his errands and ready to prepare a fine meal: 'A fine job shopping! I got just what I wanted ...' (273). The cook even nods to his status as a slave when he worries aloud about being punished for his tardiness: 'Damn, my back's already sore!' (275). At 753–774, the Senex announces his arrival by complaining about the trials and tribulations of old age such as his painfully slow gait (753–755), his lack of youthful vigour (756–759), and the various ailments with which his body is wracked: 'I could name every last one of them, but that'd take too long' (760). At 966–989, Messenio delivers his show-stopping musical meditation on slavery and explicitly self-identifies as a Good Slave: 'Others can do as they think is best for them; I'll be as I ought to be. That's my rule: to be blameless and always at

Master's beck and call' (981–982). These examples all illustrate a central function of the monologue in Roman Comedy, namely, to make it as easy as possible for the audience to quickly contextualize a stock character, connect with them, and imagine the situation from their point of view.

c) Asides; role-playing

Closely related to monologues are asides. These are usually brief, direct communications with the audience, which (funnily enough) none of the other characters are able to hear, even if they happen to be standing right next to the speaker. Asides allow the *dramatis personae* to 'press pause' and break out of the story for a moment in order to offer insider commentary. They might serve as transitions between scenes or be interwoven among dialogue. Either way, they are powerful metatheatrical tools. Slater (1985: 160) deftly explains their functions as follows:

> The aside . . . effects a profound theatrical transformation of any scene wherein it is employed as it, momentarily or for a more extended period, gives us a double vision of the scene. Sometimes this double vision can be inside and out, the characters' thoughts as opposed to their external behavior, but the aside in Plautus is by no means limited to this simple use. The aside can set source against parody, type against variation. Always it is a reminder of the special nature of communication in drama that allows us to receive two or more messages simultaneously.

Fittingly, the character who delivers the most asides in *Menaechmi* is Peniculus the parasite. A 'professional' flatterer, his *modus operandi* is cultivating personal connections and shaping the narrative through persuasive speech. His wry running commentary serves a number of important metatheatrical functions including: (1) fostering his alliance with the audience, (2) contributing to the comedy's distinctive satirical tone, and (3) providing a 'double vision' of the scene by offering a simultaneous parallel account of the action. The parasite filters our very first impression of Menaechmus E and, by extension, his wife. Peniculus deflates some of the painfully awkward tension in this scene by reframing their tragic marital discord as a comic nuisance to *his* lifestyle: 'He may think he's bad-mouthing his wife, but I'm the one taking it in the jaw. If he dines out, he punishes my stomach, not his wife' (125–126). Peniculus continues to cast a knowing, cynical side-eye to the audience in all of his scenes, modelling reception of the plot and adding sarcastic texture to the tone. In moments rife with irony, he calls out Erotium for her use of flattery to exploit his patron ('Aw, there's nothing sweeter than a prostitute with a target in her sights', 193) and later criticizes Menaechmus E for his life choices and money mismanagement ('By my accounting, those four minae just lost their lives', 206).

Asides can also be used to signal role-playing in a comedy. Plautus frequently has his characters adopt different personae in order to achieve a particular goal, and asides are valuable vehicles for indicating this to the audience (Cf. *Asinaria* 446–451; *Casina* 685–688; *Miles Gloriosus* 1066). Menaechmus S uses the aside in this way at 831–832, when he announces his plan to play mad: 'That gives me an idea. Since they've already declared me insane, why not just go with the flow and scare them away?' At 846–847, he drops the act with us, and pauses a moment to strategize: 'Now I'm stuck. If I don't come up with some plan, they're sure to carry me off to their house.' At 853, he congratulates himself on the success of his performance: 'Nice work in disposing of that piece of work! And now for this human garbage . . .' And at 876–881 he reiterates that the whole thing was just an act (got it?) and calls for the audience's complicity: 'Tell me, are those two who forced a perfectly sane person like me to go nuts finally out of sight? And shouldn't I go straight to the ship while it's safe? I've one favour to ask you all: if the old man returns don't point out my getaway route to him!' (876–881). In addition to serving a basic narrative purpose, these asides foster a special collaborative relationship between their speakers and the audience. As Slater (1985: 159–60) notes, 'the audience is privileged to hear the actors discuss among themselves the fine-tuning of a performance. Given the camaraderie between players and audience implied by the very nature of the aside, the audience in this situation therefore has the feeling that it participates in the creation of the play.'

In addition to these broadly applicable functions, asides are especially useful here in *Menaechmi* for their ability to spotlight the Mistaken Identity Bit in action. Just as the characters begin to get more and more confused by the goings-on, asides offer clarity to the audience. They provide a space in which the characters can articulate exactly how they are misinterpreting the scene. For example, when Peniculus spies a garland-wearing, *palla*-toting Menaechmus S leaving Erotium's house, he logically – if erroneously – deduces that his patron has partied without him: 'So the feast's finished, the wine's been imbibed, and the parasite's been ostracized! And now it's off to the embroiderer's with the pashmina! By Hercules, I'm not the man that I am, if I don't avenge this injustice with sweet, sweet revenge. Oh, just you watch me, you!' (469– 472). At 478–479, he continues to complain to the audience, revealing his mounting misapprehension as well as his fury. By 486, he cannot hold himself back any longer and he finally explodes at the wrong twin. These play-by-play asides underline precisely how the misunderstanding unfolds.

The very last aside in *Menaechmi* is arguably its most important. When Messenio solves the mystery of the mistaken identicals, he shares it with the audience first: 'Immortal gods! Am I looking at what I've looked forward to for so long? Unless I'm mistaken, these two are identical twins! And according to their stories, they were fathered by the same father and hail from the same country! I'll call my master aside. Menaechmus!' (1081–1084). In this way, the slave further strengthens his heroic status and cements his relationship with the audience, being the first to join those of us 'in the know'. He can now milk the final recognition scene for all it's worth, laying on the dramatic irony to which he is finally privy.

d) Eavesdropping scenes

Eavesdropping scenes function in much the same way that asides do. In fact, a character might deliver an aside whilst simultaneously eavesdropping on a fellow *dramatis persona*, as Peniculus does when he overhears Menaechmus E ranting about his wife (125–126) or when he spies Menaechmus S coming out of Erotium's house (465). An eavesdropping scene refers to any set-up in which one or more characters observes and comments upon the behaviour of another character, who has yet to detect their presence. It can be an individual sharing his or her take on the proceedings with the audience via mini-monologue(s), or it can involve multiple eavesdroppers gossiping among themselves through dialogue. The upshot is effectively the same in both cases: Like asides – and monologues, more broadly – eavesdropping scenes continue to amplify the comedic tone, the narrative layering, and the metatheatrical bond between characters and audience.

On this last point, in particular, eavesdropping scenes connect characters and audience in a whole new way. They explicitly cast the eavesdropper(s) as 'audience', watching and interpreting the action like a kind of play-within-a-play. In this way, the eavesdropper(s) perform reception, shaping, reflecting and transfiguring the external audience's view of the story. Internal and external audiences bond over their shared roles as 'voyeurs'.

Menaechmi features several eavesdropping scenes – Peniculus spying on Menaechmus E at 125–126 and on Menaechmus S at 465–485, the *senex* and doctor observing Menaechmus E from a distance at 898 – but the most memorable of all is arguably the extended eavesdropping scene in which Peniculus and the *matrona* stand by and listen in as Menaechmus E delivers a thirty-line confession (in song!) in which he explicitly admits to evading, cheating on, and stealing from his wife (571–601). The snooping is premeditated and, from what Menaechmus E has already told us about the *matrona*, a pattern of behaviour with her. Wife and parasite position themselves just out of Menaechmus E's line of sight in order to entrap him: 'Quiet down, now. I promise you. Just follow me over this way and you'll catch him red-handed ... Let's slip on over here and draw a bead on our prey' (561–570). Hoping to discover some proof of his guilt, they couldn't have anticipated such a stunning (and specific!) confession:

Menaechmus E   May the gods damn that man
  Who's ruined my day of play!
  And they may as well damn me too
  For ever setting foot in the forum!
  Yes, my day of play's been wasted!
  A tasty luncheon made to order,
  A tastier mistress left in waiting . . .
  The minute I was finished
  I high-tailed in right on out of the forum.
  She's angry, no doubt about that,
  But I'll beat that rap with the pashmina –
  Yes, the one that I stole from my wife and gave to Erotium today!
Peniculus (*to Matrona*)   Did you get that?
Matrona (*to Peniculus*)   I got it alright – I'm married to a bum.
Peniculus (*to Matrona*)   Heard enough?
Matrona (*to Peniculus*)   More than enough!

                                                    596–603

These lines underscore both the comic absurdity of the eavesdropping scene and its performance dimension. In the first place, Menaechmus E is standing in the middle of the street . . . singing . . . and sharing intimate details of his personal life. Further stretching the limits of realism, he doesn't see his wife, the one person he shouldn't be saying all this in front of, standing just a few feet away from him. Peniculus and the *matrona* are hardly inconspicuous. They may move off to the side, crouch down, or turn their backs to him, but their bodies remain *clearly* visible both to the audience and to Menaechmus E. The only reason he can't see them is adherence to convention. The rules of this theatrical world dictate that characters can be just a few feet apart from each other and only see or hear one another when the playwright permits it. Unfortunately, because of the lack of stage directions, we cannot reconstruct the reactions of wife and parasite during Menaechmus E's *canticum*. We can be sure, though, that the actors would have taken full advantage of this rich opportunity for spirited pantomime. However they may have manifested it, their body language must have reflected the outrage they voice when they finally confront Menaechmus E at 605.

Plautine language

Plautus has a distinctive comedic voice, which sets his work apart from that of other authors and genres. A product of the late third / early second centuries BCE, its phonology, morphology, syntax and lexicon are older than and strikingly different from the standardized 'Classical Latin' (*c.* 87 BCE–17 CE) of later authors like Cicero and Caesar. Plautine language comprises a wide variety of archaic forms and terms, contemporary street slang, Graecisms, tragic-epic-legalistic-ritualistic grandiloquence and plain old made-up words that just sound funny.[4] Because his plays generally depict everyday people having everyday conversations, we are tempted to take them as evidence of how ordinary Romans actually spoke in Plautus' time. As Karakasis (2019: 161) rightly cautions, however, Plautus' language is a 'literary construction, a *Kunstsprache*, and, therefore, it can by no means be considered as a pure reflection of everyday colloquialism'.

To add depth and dynamism to his dialogue, Plautus experiments with having his characters speak in different stylistic registers. Karakasis (2019: 166–7) observes, for example, that low-status characters are more likely to use colloquialisms than their high-status counterparts. Plautus plays with this idea in *Menaechmi*, when Cylindrus makes a casual observation about Menaechmus E one minute ('He's an absolute card when his wife isn't around', 318), and a moment later, switches into the lofty language of tragedy ('And you should just go . . . straight in and take your place at the table while these victuals wend their way to Vulcan's violence', 329–330). This kind of verbal *variatio* keeps the dialogue fresh and surprising and adds unexpected splashes of colour to the character portraits.

Plautus is intensely intentional about his word choice, right down to his use of expletives. When a character curses, the playwright employs distinctive linguistic markers to differentiate between male and female speech.[5] '*Ecastor*', for example, is the go-to swearword for the women in this play (Erotium and the *matrona* used it at least seven times)[6], while the men favour '*hercle*' (between both Menaechmi, Peniculus, Messenio,

Cylindrus, the *senex*, the *doctor*, and even the [mostly!] mute slaves, the word is used upwards of forty-seven times)[7]. In many ways, the care that Plautus applies to the curse words here in *Menaechmi* elegantly – if somewhat ironically – encapsulates his devotion to dialogical detail throughout his work.

What truly makes Plautus' language shine, however, is his passion for wordplay. His dialogue skips along, punctuated by puns, alliteration, finely tuned poetry, utter gibberish, and other forms of verbal fireworks designed to catch the listener's ear and add sparkle to the storytelling. The underlying voice that emerges is jaunty, clever, accessible, arcane, unreservedly ridiculous and enthusiastically artful. Fontaine (2009: 252) helpfully enumerates many of the rich and varied lexical tricks that Plautus keeps tucked up his sleeve:

> 'Funny' words can often be found in puns, and often as (a) the final word of a line, (b) one of two seemingly repeated words, which may mask a parechesis, including equivocations, mondegreens, and transliterated Greek words, and as (c) words whose morphemes can be reanalyzed to suggest a different or nonce meaning based on putative analogy (e.g., *co-nivent* ~ **con-ivent; ad-ulescens* ~ **adul-esc-ens*). They are often introduced by (a) riddling expressions, (b) catchwords, (c) visual cues, (d) patterned sequences of words (e.g., *graecissat. . . atticissat. . . sicilicissitat*), including the 'polar double-riddle' pun, which produces two puns rather than one (e.g., *Satyrio* :: **Essurio* ~ **Saturio*), (e) misleading verbal setup, (f) repartee, (g) code switching, (h) proper names, (i) structural, syntactic ambiguities, (j) transitions from one thought to another, and of course they may be found in combinations of any of these. Some of Plautus' 'funny' words involve calques, or loan translations, of Greek words known from comedy (e.g., *adul-esc-ens* ~ ψωμ-ο-κόλαξ), and more of these no doubt await future discovery.

A proper study of wordplay in *Menaechmi* would fill an entire monograph in its own right. For our purposes, let us examine a few stand-out cases that exemplify his style here and across his corpus.

In addition to announcing the ludic context and plot of the play, the Prologue is explicitly tasked with introducing and drawing attention to

Plautus' voice: 'I'm also here to present Plautus to you – with my voice [*lingua*], not my hands, that is!' (3). He accomplishes this by means of both the story he is telling, and the language with which he tells it. The Prologue fires off a starburst of Plautine pyrotechnics right in his opening speech, notably with the patterned sequence '*graecissat* . . . *atticissat* . . . *sicilicissitat*' (11–12), the made-up coinage '*sicilicissitare*' (12), the metapoetic word play on metrical and literal feet (*pedibus*, 49), and, of course, the central pun of the whole *damn* comedy, the name of the city itself (*Epidamnum*, 51). The audience is in for a Plautine play, all right, and they can expect more zingers like these, along with the familiar plot points and stock characters they know and love.

Indeed, Plautus even weaves wordplay into his characters' names. Of the characters with given names – as opposed to those who are just referred to by their character types (i.e. *senex, matrona, ancilla, medicus*, etc.) – three stand out for their onomastic wordplay: Erotium, Cylindrus and Peniculus. As we noted in the last chapter, Erotium's name is a diminutive form of the Greek word *eros,* meaning 'Little Love' or 'Lovey-Wuvy.' In addition to evoking the nature of her profession and, let's be honest, just sounding silly, it also allows Plautus to prominently feature a Graecism. In so doing, he renders the prostitute more foreign and exotic – especially when compared to the emphatically Roman (Latin) *matrona* – and also nods to the Greek New Comic tradition in which he is participating. Cylindrus is another Greek word, meaning 'cylinder', 'roller' or 'rolling pin'. The name effectively identifies him as cook, and yet Plautus *chose* to give him a distinctive name rather simply calling him *coquus*. The whole purpose of Cylindrus' name, then, is to set up a joke; it turns him into a walking, talking culinary pun. The playwright fully exploits this at 295–296, when Menaechmus S shouts: 'I don't care if you're Cylinder [*Cylindrus*] or Coriander [*Coriendrus*] – I just want you to get lost!'

Without question, the most versatile name in *Menaechmi* is Peniculus. His name has multiple meanings in both Latin *and* Greek and so offers a treasure-trove of bon mots. As we noted in the last chapter, Peniculus is a diminutive form of the Latin word *penis* which can mean either 'Little Dick' or 'Little Sponge' / 'Spongeling'. Plautus, of course, takes full advantage of its dual meaning in the parasite's opening lines: 'The Young Men have nicknamed me Peniculus ... because I always wipe the dinner table clean' (77–78). As Fontaine (2009: 105) observes, Peniculus is also the diminutive Greek word for 'toupee' making him 'Little Toupee Man', or 'Darling Mr. Headpiece.' We can't know for sure whether his costume incorporated a toupee, but Peniculus' name suggests that it may well have been an outstanding aspect of his appearance and/or comportment. Plautus thus exploits the bilingual, multimodal dimensions of the diction in order to render his parasite as ridiculous as possible.

These examples represent just a small sample of the dexterous and dazzling language that makes *Menaechmi* sing. In addition to underlining the playwright's obvious delight in wordplay, they underscore the importance of reading the text in the original Latin whenever possible or choosing a translation that strives to capture this essential aspect of Plautine Comedy.

Visual gags and physical comedy

When we read a script, it is all too easy to lose sight of the visual elements of a play. Very often – and especially in a classroom setting – we reflexively read plays as books rather than performances. We have to remind ourselves that the words on the page only tell about half of the story, that spectacle played an equal, if not more important role in shaping the audience's reception and overall experience of a drama. Like all of Plautus' plays, *Menaechmi* is full of lively physical comedy and visual gags. These dynamic displays are every bit as fundamental to Plautine comedy as the stock characters, settings and plot points that have come to define it. Let us take a closer look at some examples now.

In earlier chapters we explored how Menaechmus E's opening monologue and subsequent dialogue with Peniculus shape our first impression of him; his brashness and blustering cast him in quite an unflattering light. I would argue that the playwright mediates the 'tragedy' of Menaechmus E's words with the 'comedy' of his appearance. Injecting instant comic relief, Plautus playfully parades his protagonist on stage in women's clothing (i.e. the wife's *palla*). Cross-dressing was, of course, a regular feature of Roman Comedy; male actors routinely performed female roles. This is a different kind of 'drag show', however. As Callier (2014), among others, has observed, 'such works play on the incongruity of the male body in female costume in order both to transgress and to confirm gender norms while making the audience laugh'.[8] In other words, cross-dressing is a classic way to comically destabilize a hero's identity and authority.

Menaechmus E first mentions the *palla* at line 130: 'Take a look at this pashmina (*hanc...pallam*) I "kidnapped" from the wife. It's soon to be my whore's'. It is very likely that he is wearing the garment when he says this. Peniculus seems to confirm as much when he meets Menaechmus S later on: 'But didn't I see you coming out of your house wearing (*indutum*) that full-length pashmina?' (512–513). At 145, Menaechmus E appears to be modelling the mantle:

> **Menaechmus E** Check this out [*age me aspice*]: remind you of anything?
> **Peniculus** What's with the get-up?

The titular twin explicitly invites Peniculus – and us – to take a good long *look* at him here (*age me aspice*). *This* is our hero. In all of his glory. The *adulescens* seizes the 'spotlight' and strikes a conspicuously comic pose. Indeed, when Menaechmus E reveals the *palla* to Erotium shortly thereafter, Peniculus even encourages his patron to do a little dance in it (197). Dancing, however, is apparently the line that Menaechmus E will not cross: 'Me dance? Damn! Are you nuts?' (198). He may be in the doghouse with his wife, he may be out in broad daylight wearing stolen women's clothing, but by Hercules he has *some* dignity! A trivial joke in the grand scheme of things, this visual gag nonetheless goes a long way toward setting the cheeky tone of the comedy and establishing the ethos of one of its main characters.

In addition to gags such as this, *Menaechmi* also prominently features lively physical comedy. In the absence of stage directions, it is all but impossible to fully reconstruct the original movements of the stage action. Occasionally, we can glean brief glimpses of stock routines or gestures – such as door-knocking and cloak-tossing – from dialogue or cross-references to similar scenes in other plays. The rest we have to imagine for ourselves.

Door-knocking is a time-honoured farcical routine.[9] As noted in chapter 1, the backdrop of every extant New Comedy comprises a street in front of two or three houses. The set, then, was another formulaic feature of the genre; doors were a predictable and prominent presence, a kind of 'stock character' in their own right. Approaching and interacting with a door in a distinctive way offered actors a fun comedic opportunity. In addition to playful physical comedy, the bit could also be used to illuminate something about the character doing the knocking and/or the relationship between the characters on either side of the door. *Menaechmi* features a prime example of this at 176–180, when the parasite and his patron eagerly approach Erotium's door:

Peniculus   Time for me to batter down [*ferio*] the door?
Menaechmus E   Batter away [*feri*]. Er, hold on a second [*vel mane etiam*].
Peniculus   What? That second will put a hold on my drinking cup!
Menaechmus E   Knock nicely [*placide pulta*].
Peniculus   What? You think her door's made out of Dixie Ware [*Samiae*]?
Menaechmus E   Hold it, by Hercules! Look, she's coming out on her own [*eapse eccam exit*].

Peniculus' use of *ferio* ('batter down') here is striking (pun intended). It suggests that the actor is preparing to make a hyperbolic gesture of some sort, perhaps winding his arm around in circles or gearing up to hurl his entire body at the door. The action contributes to his cartoonish characterization; the parasite's appetite is so prodigious that he would barrel down a door just to get at the feast on the other side. Menaechmus E is similarly driven toward Erotium. Consumed by passion, he uses the same word in the imperative (*feri*) to command Peniculus to ram the door down. Barely a metrical beat later, however, Menaechmus E suddenly has a change of heart and stops the parasite in his tracks (*vel mane etiam*). One can imagine the potential for physical comedy here: perhaps Peniculus charges headlong into the door only to come to an abrupt, screeching halt culminating in a pratfall; perhaps he makes clownish contact (splat!); perhaps he comes within a hair's breadth of the door and demonstrates unexpected agility. Whatever way he interacts with the door, Peniculus' focus remains firmly fixed on what is behind it: 'What? That second will put a hold on my drinking cup!' Menaechmus E tells him to 'knock nicely' (*placide pulta*), a dramatic departure from his earlier exhortation. At this point, Peniculus delivers the punchline, the joke that the whole door-knocking bit has been leading up to: 'What? You think her door's made out of Dixie Ware [*Samiae*]?' The reference to 'Samian Ware' – or 'Dixie Ware' in Christenson's version – has a double meaning which is easily lost in translation. It alludes to the Greek Island of Samos, which was infamous for producing inexpensive, shoddy pottery as well as for its association with prostitutes in New Comedy (i.e. Chrysis in Menander's *Samia*, the titular sisters in Plautus' *Bacchides*, and Thais in Terence's *Eunuchus* all hail from Samos). Calling the door 'Samian', then, implies that it – and, by extension, the prostitute behind it – is 'chintzy' and 'cheap'. This is the precise moment when Erotium makes her grand entrance. In contrast to the men's dithering with the door, she simply opens it and steps right on out (*eapse eccam exit*). In this classic example of a door-knocking bit, the door functions as a focal point of physical comedy. Characters can engage with it in various and varying ways (e.g. battering it down vs 'knocking nicely') while confirming salient information their personalities in the process. Through their interactions with the door, Plautus reinforces Peniculus' gluttony, Menaechmus E's libidinousness, and Erotium's 'Samian' nature.

While the dialogue explicitly signals this stock routine here, other times it is silent about the characters' behaviour. In these moments, convention may be able to offer some suggestions about the staging. As

Cardoso (2019: 122) observes, 'a notorious example is the humorous depiction of the gesture of throwing on a cloak as typical for the running slave character in *Capt.* 778–80 (see also *Ep.* 194–5; *Ph.* 844–5). On the basis of this, the audience may expect the staging of such movement whenever this stock character appears.' While we cannot assume that all slaves toss their cloaks every time they run in Plautine Comedy, the convention does open up the *possibility* in each instance. Perhaps Messenio tosses a cloak over his shoulder before impetuously charging forward to save his 'master' from his assailants at 1009–1010: 'You can count on me to assist and rescue you! I'll die first myself before I allow you to die!' Perhaps he just dives directly into the fray. The script doesn't stipulate the gesture, but custom does permit it. Including a cloak-toss would not affect the story in any meaningful way, but it would be a fun formulaic flourish, a kind of 'Easter Egg' for the fans of Roman Comedy to recognize and enjoy.

While not a 'routine', per se, violence is another hallmark of Plautine physical comedy. Slapstick, it turns out, has been making people laugh for thousands of years, across infinitely diverse cultures. But what is it about people injuring themselves or one another that provokes laughter? The tone and nature of these bits are notoriously difficult to pin down. Our understanding of them is further complicated by our individual socio-historical and personal biases, in addition to the lack of textual evidence. Underscoring that there is no single answer to this question, I offer one compelling explanation for this device: Freedom From Consequence. The unwritten Rules of Roman Comedy stipulate that *it will all be ok*, at least within the limited world of the play. Slaves are walloped, women are raped, frustrated lovers threaten to kill themselves, but there are no permanent scars – physical or emotional. Roman Comedy offers characters a 'safe space', a controlled context in which they can indulge their impulses without any liability. They are aware of – and continue to be motivated by the fear of – 'real world' consequences, but they never suffer any long-term, 'real world' negative effects. Like cartoon characters, they pop right back up every time metaphorical anvils fall on their heads.

Slaves, in particular, are frequent victims of stage violence, both from their fellow slaves as well as from their masters; their vigorous pummelling is often accompanied by colourful verbal assaults (e.g. *Amph.* 374–440; *Mil.* 1394–1425; *Most.* 1–83; *Pseud.* 133–229). It is impossible to determine how Plautus intended for these scenes to be performed or, for that matter, how he hoped they would be received. Perhaps the violence was meant to have serious overtones, shining a harsh light on the dark realities of slavery. Perhaps it was meant to be playful and 'cartoonish', entertaining for its choreography and funny for its lack of consequences. As Marshall (2006: 186) observes: 'The reader can choose to imagine either or both possibilities, or might never consider the issue. The spectator [on the other hand] is presented with specific actions that lead towards a particular interpretation.' He goes on to remind us that, even when influenced by the choices and resources of a production – including, of course, the delivery of the actors – diverse audience members will always have unique, personal reactions to the material. The only thing we can say for certain, then, is that violence was a fundamental feature of Roman Comedy. Its resonance must be left to individuals to decide for themselves.

Violence appears in many forms in *Menaechmi*, including vivid narrative, farcical charade and an actual skirmish. In his famous *canticum* on slavery (966–988), for example, Messenio lays bare the brutality to which slaves were routinely subjected in graphic detail. He highlights, among other cruel punishments, 'whips, chains, millstones, fatigue, famine, [and] piercing frost' (974–975). It is likely that some form of gesture or pantomime accompanied these evocative words, though the nuances of the direction and delivery are unrecoverable. In the 'madness scene' (831–881), Menaechmus S threatens the *matrona* and *senex* with histrionic hostility. He claims that Apollo is commanding him to burn out the wife's eyes (841–842) and bash in her face with his fists (848–850), adding that the god is also telling him to beat the old man with his cane (855–856), slice out his guts (858–859), run him over with a chariot drawn by wild horses (862–864), and finally to slaughter him where he stands (869). Although Menaechmus S never actually carries out these threats, his body language during this feint of madness ('His face is all twisted and his mouth's hanging open!', 833) must have been accordingly melodramatic and menacing, since he succeeds in sending the old man and his daughter running away in terror.

The most violent exchange in *Menaechmi* is the fight sequence between Menaechmus E, Messenio and the Senex's henchmen (997–1020). Duckworth (1952: 325) calls it 'one of the noisiest scenes in Plautine comedy'. The text is quite explicit about the action here. The characters effectively narrate what they are doing while they are doing it: 'Rip out the eye of that guy who has you by the shoulder' (1011), 'Plant ... fists all over their faces' (1012), 'I've got this one's eye', 'Keep a hold on it 'til the socket shows!' (1014). On the one hand, Plautus deliberately chooses to enact the violence onstage here. He wants the audience to experience it visually as well as verbally, to make it as vivid as possible. On the other hand, the audience knows that it's all an act; they can assume that the performers are safe and that they know what they're doing. In other words, it's all fun and games precisely because there is no real risk of anyone actually losing an eye. Plautus exploits a fundamental rule of comedy here – that it is not the real world, just a fun-house mirror reflection of it – and he takes full advantage of its ludic licence. The audience knows that what they are watching is Wrong, but that *it is ok to laugh at it* in this context. The primary goal of comedy, after all, is to make us laugh. A secondary, but no less important, goal is to invite us to consider why it is that we're laughing.

This scene – along with the madness one – presents a brilliant opportunity for improvisation. As Marshall (2019: 89) observes, 'there was probably a considerable amount of improvisation in performance, with the extant texts representing transcripts assembled after a successful run, complete with variant forms of some jokes'.[10] While we can't say for certain whether the actors did or did not adlib material here, both the feint of madness and the fight sequence possess two auspicious features: (1) a premise that is simultaneously clear-cut and also flexible, and (2) space in which to experiment with this premise. Both scenes provide the actors with basic starting points and end goals (i.e. to Menaechmus S: 'pretend that you've gone crazy and do whatever it takes to scare the wife and her father away' or, to Messenio: 'fight off the attackers and protect your master at all costs') and then set them loose to contrive the funniest, most creative way to get from point A to point B. As long as the actors eventually arrive at their destination, they are free to expand or contract the action as appropriate. In this way, improvisation also involves the audience in the creative process. Tuning in to their real-time reactions (e.g. cheers and applause, distracted murmuring, booing and heckling, or [*ecastor!*] deafening silence), the actors can adapt the performance according to audience feedback. Thus, improvisation would further energize these already lively scenes by jolting them with the ineffable electricity that comes from not just live, but *living* theatre. Part of the fun is watching the actors think quickly and cleverly on their feet. Plus, there's always the 'danger' that their choices won't work. Seeing how the actors deal with jokes that fall flat can be just as entertaining as watching them succeed with those that soar. Improvisation, then, adds new and exciting layers to the scenes. The audience gets to enjoy Plautus' skillful scaffolding as well as the actors' virtuosic enhancements, uniquely tailored to them and to the moment.

A happy ending?

'No royal curse. No Trojan horse. And a happy ending of course!' So writes the great Stephen Sondheim in 'Comedy Tonight', the opening number of *A Funny Thing Happened on the Way to the Forum*, his 1962 musical mash-up of Plautus' *Pseudolus, Miles Gloriosus* and *Mostellaria*. In many ways, these lyrics succinctly capture the spirit of Roman Comedy and pinpoint what sets it apart from, say, tragedy, epic, or pretty much any other ancient genre, Greek or Roman. Roman Comedy is not about royalty (*Amphitruo*, excepted), it is about plain old everyday folks. It's not about lofty subjects like War (*Captivi*, excepted), it is about ordinary interpersonal relationships. And, of course, all's well that ends well.

And yet, of course, it's not that simple. Its predictability is the very source of its complexity. The audience has a strong hunch that the twins will eventually recognize one another, that all the comic confusion will be cleared up, that everyone will live happily ever after. How – besides allowing for improvisation – can a playwright transmute something so formulaic into something fresh and new? Where is there for the story to go, if the happy ending is so programmatically preordained? How can Plautus surprise us when the main conflict's resolution – indeed, the entire plot – is so transparent from the very beginning?

The answer is: he embraces – then exploits – the predictable, and in so doing, he creates The Unexpected. As we have seen all along, Plautus is counting on the clichés in order to establish a norm from which he can playfully, artfully deviate and return to at will. Like a conductor modulating the volume and tempo of a popular symphony, he brings a new sound to a familiar melody. Yes, the brothers will recognize one another, but Epi*damn*, it takes them a preposterously long time to do so. And, yes, everyone will live happily ever after, but what does 'happily ever after' actually mean to these characters? To Menaechmus S, it is finding his beloved brother at long last (zig); to Messenio, it is earning his freedom (zig); to Menaechmus E it is … selling all his earthly possessions, divorcing his wife, skipping town, and leaving his old life behind (ZAG!).

Let's take a closer look now at the final recognition scene. At 1050, Menaechmus S and Messenio enter arguing over the penultimate Mistaken Identity Bit: the slave is explaining how his master just freed him in return for his service in the fight; Menaechmus S is totally lost, not for the first nor the last time that day. At 1060, Menaechmus E enters from Erotium's house, rounding out the play just as he began it, by shouting at a woman offstage: 'Damn! You can swear by your own eyeballs for all I care! I never took the pashmina and the bracelet away today! Bitches!' (1059–1061). Messenio is the first to see him, though he is hardly inconspicuous:

Messenio (*to Menaechmus [S]*)   By the immortal gods! I can't believe my eyes!

Menaechmus [S] (*to Messenio*):   What do you see?
Messenio (*to Menaechmus [S]*):   Your mirror image!
Menaechmus [S] (*to Messenio*):   How's that?
Messenio (*to Menaechmus [S]*):   Your very image! You couldn't be more like you!
Menaechmus [S] (*to Messenio*):   Damn right! There's quite a likeness when I carefully examine my own appearance.
Menaechmus [E]   Young man! Hey you, yes you, my rescuer there, whoever you are!
Messenio   Yes, young man. I don't mean to bother you, but could you please tell me your name?
Menaechmus [E]   No bother at all. I owe you for all you did for me, that's for sure! My name is Menaechmus.
Menaechmus [S]   But that's my name!
Menaechmus [E]   I'm from Sicily – Syracuse.
Menaechmus [S]   That's my city and country too!
Menaechmus [E]   No! What are you saying?
Menaechmus [S]   The simple truth.

1062–1070

This goes on for another twenty lines or so before Messenio finally catches on, and it is approximately fifty-six more lines before the titular twins work it out for themselves. Messenio seizes the opportunity to leverage his knowledge for his freedom; Menaechmus S assures him, 'You'll be a free a man if you prove he's my brother' (1093–1094). Here at the climax of the play, both brothers are finally on stage together at the same time, standing face-to-identical-face as if mirror reflections of one another. Through belaboured questioning moderated by Messenio, they discover that they have the same name, they're from the same hometown, they're sons of the same father . . . and they still don't get it. Arnott (1959: 177) comments that the recognition scene is 'so prolonged that we begin to wonder whether even the Menaechmus brothers can have been so stupid'. The whole fun of the finale, then, is not about whether or not the twins will finally recognize one another, but rather how long the playwright – and the actors – can possibly sustain their implausible ignorance.

While both twins are similarly obtuse, they are not, in fact, identical in their stupidity. Menaechmus S figures out what's going on a few beats before his brother does. He asks Menaechmus E if he and his brother have always shared the same name. When Menaechmus E reveals that his brother was originally named Sosicles, Menaechmus S is finally (*finally!*) convinced: 'That's proof enough for me! I've got to give you a hug! My twin brother, hello! I'm Sosicles!' (1124–1125). Like a fairytale, it seems that all it takes to 'break the spell' is for Menaechmus E to utter his brother's real name aloud. And just like that, Menaechmus S becomes Sosicles once again. He is finally able to reclaim his own identity and relinquish that of his brother.

But what about Menaechmus E? Even with all the clues right there in front of his face – including Sosicles . . . who has the same face – he still cannot solve the mystery. His density allows Plautus to stretch the already overextended recognition scene *juuuust* a little bit further. It takes two additional rounds of questioning after Sosicles has grasped the truth, for Menaechmus E to see it. His 'magic word' is not 'Sosicles', but rather 'Teuximarcha' (1131), their mother. Her name, appropriately enough, comes from the Greek word τυγχάνω, meaning 'to chance upon'. We might roughly translate it as 'Ms. HowNiceToRandomlyBumpIntoYou'; Gratwick (1993: 241) calls her 'Mme Rencontre'. The moment Sosicles speaks her name, Menaechmus E is instantly persuaded: 'That's right. To see you, to greet you after so many years!' (1132). What is it about the mother's name that finally prevails upon him? Her name, in fact, is the one detail of the twins' backstory that was not revealed earlier in the play. All other particulars, including the father's name (Moschus), their hometown (Syracuse), etc. were disclosed either in the prologue, or through subsequent dialogue (e.g. 408–412). The mother's name, then, is a shibboleth of sorts. Not even we, the omniscient audience, are privy to this information until now. It is something only Menaechmus E's real brother would know. And now Menaechmus E can finally believe that it is really him.

Suddenly everything clicks into place. Fortified with their newfound knowledge, the twins and Messenio piece together the peculiar events of the day: *palla*, parasite, prostitute and all. The slave then reminds his master about his promise to free him. Messenio's manumission is enthusiastically endorsed by both brothers:

> **Menaechmus [E]**   His request is quite fair and reasonable, brother.
> Do it for my sake.
> **Menaechmus [S]**   You are hereby a free man.
> **Menaechmus [E]**   I'm so happy that you're free, Messenio.

1147–1148

This feel-good 'storybook ending' would have been a tidy way to conclude the comedy – the twins are reunited; the slave is freed – but Plautus still has one more trick up his sleeve. The final lines of the play announce Menaechmus E's plans to depart from Epidamnus, auction off all his belongings, and leave his wife. Contrary to the classic comedic 'happily ever after', this story ends not with a marriage, but with a divorce! Here, at the last possible moment, Plautus takes our expectations and flips them upside down one final time. And we would expect nothing less of him.

As we have seen, Plautine humour nimbly hops back and forth between convention and invention. The playwright faithfully gives his audience what they want: bits, banter and buffoonery like the Mistaken Identity Bit, whimsical metatheatre, dazzling dialogue and farcical physical comedy. Most impressive of all, he makes it look effortless, like he's just painting-by-numbers, following the Rules of Roman Comedy. In fact, his ingenuity and artistry are on display in every pun, pratfall and plot twist. As we will see in the next chapter, his distinctive style has inspired – and continues to inspire – dramatists from antiquity into the modern age.

TWINfluence on the Classical Tradition

Menaechmi is arguably Plautus' most influential play. Its imprint can be found everywhere from the Renaissance stage to the modern screen. Muecke (1987: 7) credits its stunning reach with 'historical accident in conjunction with its sustainability as a model'. In a twist of fate that might have been ripped from Plautus' own pages, *Menaechmi* was the only 'pure comedy of errors to survive from antiquity'. Its uncanny good fortune, along with the versatility of both its comedic conceit and its mechanical structure, make *Menaechmi* an eternal comedy.

This final chapter explores *Menaechmi*'s afterlife, beginning with a description of its first known revival in 1486 in Ferrara, Italy and ending with a survey of notable early modern and contemporary adaptations from around the globe. Extended discussions concentrate on the play's four most famous descendants: William Shakespeare's *The Comedy of Errors* (1594), Jean-François Regnard's *Les Ménechmes ou Les Jumeaux* (1705), Carlo Goldoni's *I Due Gemelli Veneziani* (1747), and Richard Rodgers, Lorenz Hart and George Abbott's *The Boys From Syracuse* (1938). The aim of the chapter is to identify and examine the most enduring aspects of the original Roman Comedy, and explore how later dramatists reimagined them to align with changing historical contexts and cultural aesthetics.

Early transmission and revival

Let us begin by considering how *Menaechmi* got from third-century BCE Rome to fifteenth-century CE Ferrara and onward.[1] Most scholars believe that Plautus' plays were not formally published right away, but rather that they were initially circulated as working scripts for performances. As such, the texts were altered from the very beginning by producers and actors. These emended versions floated around for another 150 years or so until the philologist M. Terentius Varro combed through the piles of plays attributed to Plautus, critically evaluated them, and canonized the official Plautine corpus.[2] According to Gratwick (1993: 34), this was followed by 'a period of neglect both theatrical and literary' that extended to the second century CE, when a new 'edition' of the twenty-one Varronian Plays (*fabulae Varronianae*) seems to have been compiled. This lost manuscript was the basis of the Ambrosian palimpsest (A) and the Palatine manuscripts (P) – our earliest extant sources of Plautus' work.

The earlier – superior – Ambrosian palimpsest was named for the Ambrosian library in Milan where it was discovered in 1815. (The term 'palimpsest' refers to a manuscript that has been effaced in some way to create space for later writing, but where traces of the original text are still evident). Contemporary scholars praised the Ambrosian palimpsest's value; the German philologist Friedrich Ritschl recognized it as 'the potentially best witness to Plautus' text'.[3] The notorious story goes that, one day, in an ill-fated attempt to enhance its legibility, the document was irreparably mutilated by chemicals. The German scholar Wilhelm Studemund famously sacrificed his eyesight in his efforts to read the letters emerging from the corrosive chemicals and transcribe them. Tarrant (1983: 303) reports, 'in its original form A contained all twenty-one 'Varronian' plays, but all or nearly all of *Amphitruo, Asinaria, Aulularia, Captivi, Curculio*, and *Vidularia* has been lost, and large parts of several other plays are now missing or illegible'. As for the state of *Menaechmi*, Gratwick (1993: 35) calls it 'a cripple among cripples' containing 'very few passages which are both continuous and soundly legible'.

The main line of transmission, then, stems from the later – inferior – Palatine manuscripts, which derive their name from the library of the Elector of the Palatinate in Heidelberg, where its two most important representatives were found. These manuscripts consist of five recensions (B, η, C, D, FZ), which in turn branch out into several medieval copies (notably E, V, J, O). By analysing their similarities, differences and marginalia, scholars have done their best to piece together the most complete and 'accurate' versions of the plays.

One of these Palatine manuscripts (D) was fortuitously brought from Germany to Italy in the fifteenth century. Discovered by Nicolas of Cusa around 1429, it contained twelve hitherto unknown Plautine comedies, including *Menaechmi*. Gratwick (1993: 36) identifies D as the 'sole and fecund source of the *Itala recensio* in the fifteenth century'. From this point on, Roman Comedy found new life in Italian schools and universities, where it was studied primarily for its linguistic, rhetorical and ethical merits (though, as a model of morality, it required a fair amount of creative licence – or outright censorship – on the part of the teachers). It soon gained prominence in both Italian and French curricula, whereby it would go on to shape the character of both countries' national theatre.[4] Future playwrights and actors – not to mention audience members – were introduced to these plots and characters in the classroom; they deepened their understanding of the genre by participating in performances in academic settings. Indeed, schools and universities were the first venues for modern productions of Roman Comedy. A student production of Terence's *Andria* in 1476 in Giorgio Vespucci's school in Florence is the earliest attested performance of Roman Comedy in the modern era. These academic events gained popularity, occurring more and more frequently throughout the 1480s. This, in turn, led to the rise of more elaborate productions in princely courts, from Ferrara to Mantua and back to where it all began, Rome itself.

Plautus, *Menaechmi*, translated perhaps by Duke Ercole I of Ferrara (1486)

This brings us to the first known revival of Plautus' *Menaechm*i on 25 January 1486 in the court of Ercole I, Duke of Ferrara, also known as Ercole d'Este.[5] The production was a landmark event for several reasons: (1) It was the first publicly performed play in Ferrara, (2) it featured lavish, spectacular staging, and, most importantly, (3) it seems to have been the first public presentation of a Roman Comedy in vernacular translation. For the first time in modern theatrical history, knowledge of Latin was no longer a prerequisite for accessing and enjoying these ancient plays. Returning to its roots, Roman Comedy could once again be popular entertainment.

The *Menaechmi* production of 1486 was designed to make a splash. It was a headlining feature of an extravagant festival held in honour of Francesco Gonzaga's visit to Ferrara prior to marrying Isabella d'Este, daughter of Ercole I. The duke spared no expense on the festivities, which included a dazzling display of fireworks among other colourful carnival entertainments. Over 10,000 people were reportedly in the audience.[6] The set was meticulously constructed with breathtaking realism, and Menaechmus S is said to have arrived on the scene in a real galley (complete with a sail!).[7] The cost of the production was estimated to be somewhere between 700 and 1000 ducats.[8] Just a few years later, in 1491, the Este family staged *Menaechmi* for a second time as part of a festival celebrating the marriage of Ercole I's son, Alfonso d'Este and Anna Sforza, daughter of the duke of Milan.

The question remains: Why *Menaechmi*? As we have seen, the play doesn't exactly present a sunny portrait of marriage. Indeed, the 'happy ending' culminates in a divorce! Ercole I could have chosen any of the twelve 'new' Plautine comedies, or any contemporary theatrical work, for that matter. Instead he chose to stage a play about a faithless husband who cheats on, steals from, and eventually leaves his wife. It seems like an odd choice for entertainment at not just one, but two wedding celebrations. I would argue that the novelty of the play – a recently rediscovered ancient text translated into contemporary Italian for the first time! – coupled with the timelessness of its plot and the carnivalesque spirit of the occasion made it the ideal candidate for performance. Like a Best Man's wedding toast in which he playfully roasts the groom, the comedy presents a Saturnalian send-up of marriage. Ultimately, it's all in good fun, adding playful, personal dimensions to these august, political events.

Ercole I became a passionate patron of the arts, elevating Ferrara's reputation as a theatrical mecca. Roman Comedy always held a special place in his heart; he may have translated some of the plays, including the first vernacular production of *Menaechmi*, and even taken on acting roles himself. As Hardin (2003–4: 256) reports, 'In all, between 1486 and 1505 Ercole had an active role in presenting at least fourteen different plays by Plautus and Terence.' Highet (1967: 133) observes that 'the noble house of Ferrara did more than any other family, and more than most European nations, for the development of the modern theatre'.[9]

The excitement generated by the 1486 production in Ferrara contributed to the rising wave of interest in Roman Comedy. Performances of Plautus and Terence, in general, and *Menaechmi*, in particular, took off across Italy and Europe. While the play continued to be staged in Latin, notably in Florence (1488) and in Rome (1502; 1511), it also received a string of vernacular productions, notably in Bologna (1491), Cesena (1492), Milan (1493) and Mantua (1502). As for the Ercole family, in keeping with tradition, they presented the play two more times at dynastic wedding celebrations: in 1502 (in Latin) on the occasion of Alfonso d'Este's second marriage to Lucrezia Borgia, and in 1528 (in French) on the occasion of Ercole II's marriage to Renata di Francia, daughter of Louis XII. Roman Comedy had found its way back into the cultural limelight.

Another watershed moment in *Menaechmi*'s history was its first printed publication. Plautus' plays were published for the first time in Venice in 1472, two years after Terence's first edition appeared in Strasbourg. The texts of Roman Comedy could now circulate widely – and authoritatively – in schools and on stages across Europe. At first, Terence's plays were better received internationally, especially in Spain and France. A staggering 520 editions of his work were published between 1470 and 1600, with a two-thirds majority of them coming from Italy and France. Plautus' comedies took a bit longer to catch on outside of Italy. In France, for example, the first Latin edition of his plays didn't appear until 1513 and the first French translation wasn't published until 1658, only a decade before Molière began staging adaptations of his plays (e.g. *L'Avare* in 1668). Candiard (2019: 327–8) offers two compelling explanations for the comparatively muted international response to Plautus' work: (1) the influence of school syllabi, which favoured Terence, and (2) the very different positions that comedy occupied in Italian and French culture. She observes that, through the patronage of Italian nobility, 'at a very early date, Roman comedy was integrated into national and local cultural life, and this allowed Italian readers and spectators to appreciate the comic efficiency of Plautus' plays'. In France, on the other hand, comedy mainly flourished in academic settings. Humanists admired these plays for their 'aesthetic poise and moral value', wherein Terence has historically outshined Plautus. Nonetheless, Plautus maintained a persistent presence in sixteenth-century *commedia erudita* ('learned comedy'). As Hardin (2003–4: 258) notes, '*Menaechmi* spinoffs such as the anonymous *Gl'Ingannati* [*The Deceived*], Bernardo (Cardinal Bibbiena) Dovizi's *La Calandra* [*The Carriage*], and G.G. Trissino's *I Simillimi* [(*The Identicals*), which, along with Agnolo Firenzuola's *I Lucidi*, one of the closest imitations of *Menaechmi*,] plotted their own special course through the road map of European theater.'

While Terence enjoyed greater esteem on printed pages and scholarly stages, Plautus found special favour among practitioners of less literary, more elastic dramatic forms, such as *commedia dell'arte*. These largely farcical and improvisational artists played a key role in Plautus' increasing traction in the theatrical tradition.[10] They looked to his comedies for inspiration on character types, *lazzi* (such as the running slave routine), and storylines.[11] *Menaechmi* was a particularly fruitful model for *commedia dell'arte*, which employed the Mistaken Identicals theme in at least twenty plots or subplots.[12] These scenarios mixed and matched new sets of doubles, such as twin Capitanos, twin Pantalones, twin girls and twin lovers. Whatever the combination, the fundamental principles of the Mistaken Identity Bit remained unchanged (see chapter 3); the comedic convention translated fluently from third-century BCE Latin to seventeenth-century CE vernacular Italian. As these comedic troupes travelled around and beyond Italy and settled in Paris, especially, they imported these characters and conceits, expanding the breadth of their influence.

It took even longer for Plautus to gain a footing in England. Continuing its string of remarkable luck – or, perhaps more accurately, building on its aggregate luck – *Menaechmi* was also the first known classical drama to appear at the English court. It was selected by Cardinal Wolsey to be performed in Latin at Hampton Court on 3 January 1527. Because King Henry VIII would be entertaining dignitaries from all over Europe, the programme had to be accessible, appropriate and, above all, impressive. *Menaechmi* was the perfect choice: the play had been steadily performed – in Italy, especially – every few years since its first revival in 1486, and its popularity was thriving, particularly among courtly audiences. (For reference, the Este family would stage it again the following year to celebrate the marriage of Ercole II and Renata di Francia.) The performance was a resounding success, according to a letter written by the Venetian secretary, Gasparo Spinelli, who was in attendance at Hampton Court. Hardin (2003–4: 259) notes, 'the king wished not just to sate, however, but to impress with sophistication (a notable Roman Comedy), and bounty, and thus to create in his guests the sense of obligation that such lavish hospitality can achieve'.[13] The play, then, continued to gather both political and popular momentum as it skyrocketed into the Renaissance. Hardin (2003–4: 263) largely credits its success in the sixteenth century to its mathematically elegant structure and its fashionable focus on the themes of Identity and Fortune:

> In a time of courtiership and self-fashioning, the play of identity must account for a large measure of *Menaechmi*'s appeal. Securing one's place, however, depended as much on one's fortune as one's identity. A familiar question of this era asks whether we live our lives through blind chance, or a sometime beneficent Fortuna, or providential grace, or individual virtù. *Menaechmi*, with a few plays like *Captivi* and *Rudens*, stands apart from Plautus's other work because it develops not

from the tricks and efforts of a clever slave, parasite, wife, or whore, but because it is so utterly a comedy of fortune.

In addition to courtly spheres, Roman Comedy continued to flourish in English schools and universities, where it soon became a staple of British curricula. Oxford and Cambridge began staging student productions of Plautus and Terence as early as 1510–11. The frequency of its academic appearances is often attributed to the play's relative wholesomeness. Simply put, as a school text, *Menaechmi* generally required less intervention (i.e. sanitization) than Plautus' other comedies. As Miola (2019: 313) notes:

> The classical playwrights who displayed so joyfully the workings of lust, avarice, and deceit on stage, of course, required careful handling for Christian students and audiences. Editors, teachers, compilers, translators, and adapters all practise elaborate strategies of containment and reformulation. The plays routinely appear with moralizing commentary, and sometimes there is a prefatory word of caution. W. B.'s English version of *Menaechmi* (1595), for example, advertises itself on the title page as 'Chosen purposely from out of the rest, as least harmful and most delightful.'

Just as they had done in Italy and France, schools and universities once again played a vital role in introducing the fundamentals of Roman Comedy to new generations of playwrights, actors and audience members, and contributing to the proliferation of its characters, plots and devices beyond their ivy-covered walls. Two of the brightest luminaries of the early modern English stage, Ben Jonson and William Shakespeare, leaned heavily on Plautus' work: Jonson's *The Case is Altered* (1597) combines narrative and structural elements from *Captivi* and *Aulularia,* while Shakespeare's *The Comedy of Errors* (1594) famously reimagines *Menaechmi* and borrows from *Amphitruo.* Let us take a closer look at *The Comedy of Errors* now, and explore the ways in which Shakespeare reincarnates the content and spirit of *Menaechmi* in sixteenth-century Elizabethan England.

William Shakespeare, *The Comedy of Errors* (1594)

Menaechmi and *The Comedy of Errors* are cut from the same cloth, a theatrical tapestry in which imitation and innovation are intricately interwoven. Just as Plautus looked to the Greeks for inspiration, Shakespeare turned to the Romans (among other sources). With its clockwork structure, formulaic plot and familiar character types, *Menaechmi* offered Shakespeare both a model with which to experiment and a springboard from which to launch into the classical tradition.

Though we know a good deal more about him than we do about Plautus, many aspects of Shakespeare's life and work remain a mystery. Hazy biographical details, such as the particulars of his education, continue to be the subject of scholarly debate. We don't know where or how he encountered Plautus' work, or to what extent he could even read Latin. The testimony of his friend and colleague, Ben Jonson, in the 1623 First Folio, suggests that Shakespeare had 'small Latin and less Greek.' Would that have been enough to fully gauge and grasp the depth and breadth of Plautus' project? The first known English translation of *Menaechmi* by William Warner wasn't published until 1595, a year after *The Comedy of Errors*' first performance. Shakespeare may have had access to an early version of Warner's text, he may have worked his way through the Latin himself or with assistance, or he may have simply heard the story second-hand in English.[14]

The sophistication of his adaptation suggests that Shakespeare rigorously engaged with *Menaechmi* in one form or another. Although it has been criticized as derivative, insubstantial and one of his more immature plays, *The Comedy of Errors* in fact displays an erudite and artful understanding of how Roman Comedy works, from its lighthearted pretences to its darker undercurrents. Though *Menaechmi* was the play's primary model, Shakespeare also drew inspiration from a variety of other sources, both ancient and contemporary. *Amphitruo's* imprint can be seen in the bard's decision to double the doubles, that is, to introduce twin slaves for twin masters. It also provided a model for the 'lock-out' scene (3.1), in which Adriana entertains Antipholus of Syracuse, thinking he is her husband.

Beyond Roman Comedy, Shakespeare's most conspicuous influences include: the works of George Gascoigne (especially *Supposes* 1575), the English comic tradition (especially stories featuring shrewish wives), and the Bible (especially Paul's Epistle to the Ephesians and Acts 19 for their depictions of Ephesus).[15] John Lyly's *Mother Bombie*, another comedy of errors, seems to have been staged around 1590 and may have been another one of Shakespeare's sources. As Dolan (1999: xxxiv) notes, 'If Shakespeare's claim to fame does not lie in inventing new stories, then perhaps it lies in his ability to identify the issues and stories of greatest appeal to a broad audience, and to create, in large part through judicious borrowing and creative recombination, especially compelling versions of popular stories.' The same, of course, could be said of Plautus. In fact, this is one of the two playwrights' most fundamental similarities; they dexterously appropriate material from others, while simultaneously transforming it and making it their own.

The Comedy of Errors tells the tale of twin brothers, who share the same name, are separated as children, and reunite as adults following mounting mayhem over mistaken identities. In other words, it's *Menaechmi Take Two: Double Trouble! (Now With Twice The Twins!).* Shakespeare's plot maps almost perfectly onto Plautus'. Indeed, the expository prologue rings some remarkably familiar bells: Once upon a time in Epidamnus, a pair of identical twin boys – both named Antipholus – were born. Their parents decided to move the family back to their homeland of Syracuse, but on the voyage, they encountered a storm at sea. A shipwreck separated the father and one son from the mother and the other. Unable to reconnect, each parent raised a twin on their own. When the father's twin turned eighteen, he went off in search of his long-lost family members and never returned. The father, Egeon, now searches for Antipholus of Syracuse, who is himself searching for Antipholus of Ephesus and their mother. His quest has brought him here to Ephesus.

Right from the start, Shakespeare makes a number of pointed allusions to the Plautine original: homonymous twins, familiar locations (Epidamnus and Syracuse), the shipwreck motif, and, most conspicuously, the search story itself. He is channelling Plautus here, establishing a clear kinship between his play and *Menaechmi*, as well as setting up an expectation that he will adhere to its model. At the same, he also begins to deviate from his prototype. Shakespeare introduces a number of innovations within the first scene alone, for example, the now prominent roles of the parents and the new setting of Ephesus. Furthermore, he has Egeon deliver the [lower case] prologue rather than an anonymous [upper case] Prologue, and the father does so in dialogue with a new character, the duke of Ephesus, as opposed to a monologue directed toward the audience. Shakespeare's most striking invention, however, is revealed in scene two: a second set of twins, who just so happen to share the same name (Dromio) and status (servant to an Antipholus). On the one hand, the bard implicitly announces his debt to *Menaechmi* here; on the other hand, he reveals his plans to radically revise it.

Much ink has been spilled contrasting these two plays. Miola (2019: 316–17) neatly summarizes the Shakespearean alterations as follows:

> The identical twins in *Menaechmi* get doubled in *Errors*, and the resulting confusions multiply exponentially. From 'Apollonius of Tyre' Shakespeare adds a frame plot that contributes missing parents, likewise split apart for many years. He transforms the *medicus* into Doctor Pinch, also a zany pedant who confidently pronounces one of the twins possessed and tries an exorcism, only to get slapped and later singed for his pains. Shakespeare transforms the female roles in Plautus' play to explore the mysteries and madness of love. He changes Erotium into the Courtesan, who provides some laughs and tells the only deliberate lie in the play. He greatly expands the nagging *matrona* into the complicated wife Adriana, who mistakes her husband for his twin, accuses him of infidelity, and receives finally a comic exposure for her jealousy ('She did betray me to my own reproof' [5.I.90]). Shakespeare adds Luciana, Adriana's sister, to provide a love interest for the single twin, and also the spherical and sweating Nell, interested in love with the wrong Dromio. And, finally, he adds Emilia, certainly a surprise to the audience, the long-lost mother of the Antipholus twins, wife to the

imprisoned Egeon, and now the Abbess who presides over the final reconciliations and reunions.[16]

Rather than focus on Shakespeare's changes to Plautus' work, however, let us instead concentrate on the aspects of the original that he chose to preserve in his adaptation: (1) Mechanical elements (in particular, composition, plot, character types and setting); (2) Thematic elements (in particular, slavery, among many others such as identity, fortune, and misogyny); (3) Stylistic elements (in particular, word play and physical comedy); and (4) Dramaturgical elements (in particular, props and actors).

The mechanical similarities between *The Comedy of Errors* and *Menaechmi* are perhaps the easiest to spot at a glance. For all their subtle differences, the plays share the same basic infrastructure, with regard to composition, plot, character types and setting. Both stories unfold over five acts, and in both cases, the focus is more or less evenly distributed between the twins. However, Shakespeare's addition of a *second set* of twins, along with a host of other new characters (e.g. the twins' mother and father, the wife's sister Luciana, etc.), escalates the potential for misapprehension and introduces new variables in need of balancing. As Rouse (1912: xiii) has pointed out, *The Comedy of Errors* has nearly three times the number of Mistaken Identity Bits that *Menaechmi* does.[17] Despite the additional threads to untangle, Shakespeare nonetheless manages to advance the action with Plautine precision and symmetry, and fit everything into the traditional Greek New Comic five-act framework that Plautus himself was working with.

The plot of *The Comedy of Errors* continues to revolve around one twin's quest to find his brother and the trouble he inadvertently stumbles into and stirs up along the way. Even though Shakespeare adds new layers to the narrative – for example, the parents' separation and reunion, or Antipholus and Dromio of Syracuse's amatory subplots with Luciana and Nell, respectively – the main plotline remains focused on the brothers' search story, and the main source of comedy continues to spring from characters confusing them with one another.

The characters themselves are all familiar faces, even the new ones in their own way. Most of the original cast is reincarnated here in one form or another: the Menaechmi twins transform into Antipholus of Syracuse and Antipholus of Ephesus; Messenio becomes Dromio of Syracuse *and* Dromio of Ephesus; the anonymous *Matrona* is finally given a name, Adriana, and a larger role in the story; by contrast, Erotium loses her name (she is simply 'the Courtesan' here), and her role is drastically diminished; the anonymous *Ancilla* becomes Luce/ Nell; and, finally, the anonymous *Medicus* becomes the famous Dr Pinch. Conspicuously absent are Peniculus, Cylindrus and the *matrona's* father. In their place, Shakespeare has introduced a new company of clowns to bolster the comedic confusion and its eventual resolution: Luciana, Solinus, Egeon, the Abbess/Emilia, Angelo the Goldsmith, Balthasar the merchant, and two other nameless merchants. Though they belong to another time and place – especially the duke and abbess – these characters nonetheless blend naturally into the landscape of Roman Comedy. They remain stock types, called upon to fulfil programmatic roles in a formulaic story without demanding substantial intellectual or emotional investment from the audience. At the same time, they do introduce new layers of pathos to the narrative – especially Luciana, Egeon and Emilia – which ultimately amplify the volume of the happy ending.

While the setting shifts from Epidamnus to Ephesus, it nonetheless retains many of its original features, most notably its status as a hybrid Graeco-Roman-Nowhere 'Plautinopolis' (see chapter 2). By choosing to locate *The Comedy of Errors* in Ephesus, Shakespeare preserves the New Comic tradition of setting the story in the Greek-ish world, wherein he can blur the boundaries between the customs of Others and those of his own people. An important Greek city in Asia Minor and one of Plautus' own go-to settings (cf. *Miles Gloriosus*), Ephesus was a perfect choice. Furthermore, like Plautus' Epidamnus, Ephesus also had a reputation as a kind of wicked wonderland, where enchanters and enchantresses (in this case, supernatural agents rather than con-artists) tried to trick and change people. It is likely that Shakespeare drew inspiration from Paul's

Epistle to the Ephesians and Acts 19, in particular, which offer vivid descriptions of Ephesus and its strange sorceries.[18]

> **Antipholus of Syracuse**   Upon my life, by some device or other
> The villain is o'erraught of all my money.
> They say this town is full of cozenage,
> As nimble jugglers that deceive the eye,
> Dark-working sorcerers that change the mind,
> Soul-killing witches that deform the body,
> Disguised cheaters, prating mountebanks,
> And many such-like liberties of sin.
> If it prove so, I will be gone the sooner.
> I'll to the Centaur, to go seek this slave.
> I greatly fear my money is not safe.
>
> 1.2.98-108[19]

Although the official setting is now Ephesus, Epidamnus is never truly far away. Its notoriety haunts the story and its name is explicitly mentioned no less than seven times throughout the play. Epidamnus – and indeed Syracuse too – are part of *The Comedy of Errors'* theatrical DNA; by calling attention to the twins' birthplace and family home as early as the prologue (1.1.39-64), Shakespeare signposts his source material. These characters *were* born in Epidamnus; it is the origin of their prototypes.

So much for the mechanical elements. Let us now turn to the plays' thematic similarities, which include the motifs of slavery, identity, fortune and misogyny to name only a few. A full analysis of any one of the these would fill – and has filled – entire book-length studies. For our purposes, let us focus on slavery, in particular, one of dominant themes in both *The Comedy of Errors* and *Menaechmi*. Already a complicated issue in Plautus' work, Shakespeare problematizes it further here. To begin with, he literally doubles Messenio's role; two Dromios offer him exponentially more opportunities to explore and exploit their status on stage. Secondly, he obscures the precise nature of the Dromios' position. Whereas Messenio is unequivocally a slave, the Dromios are alternately referred to as slaves, servants or bondmen. This blurriness corresponds to the ambiguous nature of servitude in Shakespeare's own time.[20] To bring this into sharper focus, the playwright casts a special spotlight on the violence they endure. As Hunt (1997: 31) observes:

> *The Comedy of Errors* is remarkable for the extent of the physical beatings given the Dromios as well as for the commentary on it. This is especially true when the pertinent episodes are compared with their sources in Plautus' *Menaechmi* and *Amphitruo*. The rough treatment of the Dromios and their ambiguous servant/slave status reflect similar features of Elizabethan servitude. In *The Comedy of Errors*, Shakespeare constructs the Dromios so as to condense the potential slavishness of sixteenth-century English service. The playwright's focus on de facto slavery widens to encompass the institution of marriage and the individual's ordering of his or her inner faculties.

Indeed, while Messenio discusses the violent realities of slavery in *Menaechmi* (966–989), we never actually see him on the receiving end of it, other than the skirmish into which he gallantly jumps and from which he gamely emerges unscathed. At no point is he beaten by his master or anyone else for that matter. As Hamilton (1992: 78) notes, 'beaten at nearly every turn of the plot by the contending Adriana and Antipholi, the besieged Dromios literalize the language of violence . . . not evenhandedly (Adriana suffers no injury) but in such a way as to display hierarchy senselessly victimizing the disempowered'. Meditating on his lot in life, Dromio of Ephesus delivers his own version of Messenio's *canticum* on slavery at 4.4.32-43, though with a palpably more pessimistic personal outlook:

> **Dromio of Ephesus**   I am an ass indeed; you may
> prove it by my long ears. – I have served him from
> the hour of my nativity to this instant, and have
> nothing at his hands for my service but blows.
> When I am cold, he heats me with beating; when I
> am warm he cools me with beating. I am waked
> with it when I sleep, raised with it when I sit,
> driven out of doors with it when I go from home,
> welcomed with it when I return. Nay, I bear it

on my shoulders as a beggar wont her brat, and I
think when he hath lamed me, I shall beg with it
from door to door.

The final blow, so to speak, is the ending itself. Whereas Messenio is
the main arbiter in *Menaechmi's* recognition scene, the Dromios are
stripped of this power in *The Comedy of Errors*. It is the duke, Solinus,
who initiates the recognition sequence, whereupon the rest of the
characters collaboratively work it out amongst themselves. In these
final revelatory moments, the Dromios more closely resemble the
Menaechmi brothers in their obtuseness than Messenio for his
cleverness. And despite the twin Dromios' joyful reunion with one
another, at the end of the day, at the end of the play, they are still slaves,
while Messenio is freed. All of these deliberate deviations from the
ancient comedy allow Shakespeare to explore the subject of slavery in
his own time. For all their differences, then, Messenio and the Dromios
actually serve similar functions in their respective plays: they are both
indispensable instruments of contemporary social commentary.

In addition to their mechanical and thematic points of contact with
one another, *The Comedy of Errors* and *Menaechmi* also share a number
of stylistic elements in common. In particular, they both rely heavily on
fanciful word play and farcical physical comedy to get a laugh. When
Antipholus of Syracuse accuses the wrong Dromio of stealing the
money he gave him, the slave responds with a particularly Plautine pun:

Antipholus of Syracuse   Now, as I am a Christian, answer me
   In what safe place you have bestowed my money,
   Or I shall break that merry sconce of yours
   That stands on tricks when I am undisposed.
   Where is the thousand **marks** thou hadst of me?
Dromio of Ephesus   I have some **marks** of yours upon my pate,
   Some of my mistress' **marks** upon my shoulders,
   But not a thousand **marks** between you both.
   If I should pay your Worship those again,
   Perchance you will not bear them patiently.

                                                    1.2.78-87

The double meaning of 'marks' here, referring both to currency and bruises, echoes the type of linguistic humour found at *Menaechmi* 978, when Messenio hopes for *verba* (words) rather than *verbera* (beatings). In this way, both playwrights use linguistic levity to undercut the threat of physical violence. This is just one example of the hundreds of puns that run throughout *The Comedy of Errors*, some more poignant like this one, others purely playful like Dromio of Syracuse's catalogue of corporeal puns describing his amorous encounter with Nell (3.2.77-172). As Mowat and Werstine (1996: xxi) remark, 'such wide-ranging puns are so characteristic of the language of this play – particularly the conversations that involve either Dromio – that the play's dialogue needs to be listened to carefully if one is to catch all its meanings'.

As far as physical comedy goes, like *Menaechmi*, *The Comedy of Errors* also derives much of its humour from slapstick and other elements of farcical stage action. Shakespeare draws directly from the Plautine playbook when he incorporates 'door-knocking' bits – like the ones that punctuate the extended lock-out scene (3.1) – as well as stage violence like the reimagined fight sequence in which Antipholus of Ephesus is restrained by Dr Pinch's men and taken away by an officer (4.4.112-139). His most breathtaking (pun intended) adaptation of Plautine physical comedy, however, occurs at 4.2.34-36, when Dromio of Syracuse dashes toward Adriana to get money for his master's bail. Here Shakespeare nods to Plautus' 'running slave' routine in three clever ways: On one level, he explicitly announces the routine in the dialogue:

Luciana   How hast thou lost thy breath?
Dromio of Syracuse   By running fast.
Adriana   Where is thy master, Dromio? Is he well?

On a second level, he reveals a glimpse of the accompanying choreography (i.e. running fast, gasping for air). On a third, ever more playful level, he activates the etymology of Dromio's name – δρόμο – the Greek word for 'running' or 'race course'. By naming him at this precise moment, within the same breath as his 'master', Shakespeare literally brings the ancient running slave to life on the Elizabethan stage.

Last, but not least, let us consider some of the dramaturgical parallels between *Menaechmi* and *The Comedy of Errors*, in particular their use of props and actors. As we have seen, props can play a vital role in executing the 'Mistaken Identity Bit'. In *Menaechmi*, for example, talismans such as the cloak (*palla*) and the bracelet (*spinter*) help the audience track the twins' movement from one scene to the next. All the audience needs to do is remember which brother had which props in his possession last. At the same time, these talismans also contribute to the characters' confusion. The characters see someone who looks like the Menaechmus that they know carrying an object that they recognize, and they naturally assume that he is *their* twin. Conversely, when they see a Menaechmus *without* an object that he *should* have – who, furthermore, denies knowing anything about said object – it escalates the comic chaos even further. Without the audience's wide-lens view of the story, the props seemingly corroborate the characters' myopic misapprehension.

Shakespeare understood the special utility of talisman props in comedies of errors. Instead of a *palla* and *spinter*, however, he chose to use a gold chain, a gift from Antipholus of Ephesus to his wife. Much ink has been spilled on the meaning behind this decision. Henze (1971), for example, offers a compelling interpretation linking the symbolism of the chain to the theme of personal freedom in the play. Whatever Shakespeare's reasoning, he recognized the prop's explosive potential. The talisman is first mentioned at 2.1.111, when Adriana discusses it with Luciana: 'Sister, you know he promised me a chain. / Would that alone o' love he would detain, / So he would keep fair quarter with his bed.' This sets the stage for the (ahem) chain of events that follows. As Baldwin (1965: 90–1) notes, 'in the third act the chain device become functional, and is developed in the fourth to lead to the catastrophe in the fifth'. Structurally, the *palla* and *spinter* perform the exact same roles in the final two acts of *Menaechmi*.

Finally, let us turn to the matter of actors. By Shakespeare's time, most European theatrical forms had abandoned the use of masks. On the one hand, this gave actors greater visibility and freedom of expression. On the other hand, it complicated certain dramaturgical illusions, for example, cross-gender casting and the twins' similitude. If the twins in *The Comedy of Errors* were played by different actors, without masks they could no longer be truly identical. While costuming and makeup can go a long way toward suggesting their resemblance, the effect would never be as convincing as actors sharing the same face. Miola (1994: 21) notes, 'we do not know exactly how Shakespeare's company cast the original performances of *The Comedy of Errors*, but we do know that the challenge of finding look-alikes proved too much for Ben Jonson, who abandoned his errors play, a version of *Amphitruo*, because he "could never find two so like others that he could persuade the spectators they were one"'. To solve this problem, Shakespeare returned to Plautus himself. He arranged the structure of *The Comedy of Errors* so that, like in *Menaechmi*, the Antipholus and Dromio twins can in fact be played by the same pair of actors right up until the final recognition scene, at which point they interact with identically costumed doubles. If a production wished, the doubles could even obscure their faces by simply positioning their backs to the audience during the denouement. While not necessary, double-casting the twins would make the starring roles even more fun for the actors to play and for the audience to follow.

Based on their mechanical, thematic, stylistic and dramaturgical similarities and differences, *The Comedy of Errors* and *Menaechmi* are more like 'fraternal' than 'identical' twins. Long-lost brothers finally reunited on the Elizabethan stage, they share an undeniable family resemblance, while at the same time possessing their own distinct identities and stories.

Jean-François Regnard, *Les Ménechmes, ou Les Jumeaux* (1705)

Turning our gaze now from sixteenth-century England to eighteenth-century France, let us examine another eminent adaptation: Jean-François

Regnard's *Les Ménechmes, ou Les Jumeaux* ('*The Menaechmi or The Twins*').
Regnard was a celebrated playwright, widely respected as France's best
comic poet after Molière. He wrote several short plays and farces in the
commedia dell'arte tradition for the Théâtre des Italiens in Paris, and twenty-
three comedies in verse, including *Les Ménechmes*, for the prestigious La
Comédie-Française, the National French Theatre created by Molière
himself and founded by Louis XIV on 8 August 1680. To date, La Comédie-
Française remains the oldest active theatre company in the world.

Regnard's own life story is astonishingly reminiscent of Plautine
comedy, complete with adultery, shipwrecks, pirates, slaves, cooks,
courtesans and even a surprise reunion.[21] Born to a wealthy *bourgeoise*
family and raised on the classics in school, he set out as a young man of
twenty to travel to Italy. In Bologna, he fell madly in love with a certain
Elvire, who was inconveniently married to a Monsieur de Prade at the
time; they carried on an adulterous affair for two years. On 4 October
1678, at the age of twenty-two, he was sailing back to France (along with
his friend Monsieur aux Cousteaux de Fercourt, Madame Elvire de Prade,
. . . and her husband), when a storm hit and shipwrecked their boat. The
travellers were captured by Algerian pirates, sold into slavery, and
subsequently taken to Constantinople where they served in the household
of one Achmet-Thalem. As luck would have it, Regnard, Cousteaux de
Fercourt and Elvire were sold together; Monsieur de Prade was separated
from the group at the slave market in Algiers and was no longer in the
picture. In captivity, Regnard managed to parlay his cooking skills into a
relatively privileged position as the Gourmet French Chef of his master.
He stirred up trouble with Achmet-Thalem, however, when he caught the
attention of some courtesans in his harem. Like a *Deus ex machina*, the
French consul in Constantinople arrived with ransom money and
rescued Regnard, along with his beloved Elvire and dear friend Cousteaux
de Fercourt. The group joyfully returned to Paris, where Regnard and
Elvire began planning their wedding and future together. Alas, eight
months later, Monsieur de Prade, presumed dead, suddenly reappeared
on the scene very much alive and accompanied by the two monks who
had managed to buy him back from his slave owner. De Prade, now

happily reunited with Elvire, decided to celebrate a second wedding with his lawful wife, leaving Regnard alone and utterly devastated.

This latest shocking turn of events proved too much for the young author. He left Paris and took to the open roads and seas once again with a small cadre of friends including Cousteaux de Fercourt. In his travel journal, *Voyage en Flandre, en Hollande, en Danemark et en Suède*, which is equally if not more famous than his plays, he describes his expedition through northern Europe. He made it as far as Lapland, where on 22 August 1681 he carved four Latin verses into the rock of a remote mountain which he and his companions named Metavara, commemorating the scope of his journey:

Gallia nos genuit; vidit nos Africa; Gangem
Hausimus; Europamque oculis lustravimus omnem;
Casibus et variis acti terraque marique,
Hic tandem stetimus, nobis ubi defuit orbis.

– De Fercourt, De Corberon, Regnard
(Anno 1681, die 22 Augusti)[22]

Gaul (France) bore us; Africa saw us;
We drank the Ganges' waters; We gazed upon all of Europe with our eyes;
And driven by changing fortunes both on land and sea
Here at last we stood, where for us the world vanished.

– De Fercourt, De Corberon, Regnard
(22 August 1681)

Having finally satisfied his wanderlust, he returned to France, where he spent the remainder of his days writing plays, entertaining friends and dignitaries, and dividing his leisure time between his house in Paris and his Chateau de Grillon in Dourdan. He never married, and he kept with him until his death on 4 September 1709 the chain that had shackled him during his time as a slave.

Like Shakespeare, Regnard's work is deeply indebted to Plautus; the French comic poet is even more explicit than the English bard about acknowledging his source. Not only does Regnard preserve the original names of the twins and, by extension, the original title, but he even features Plautus himself as a character in the prologue, which he divides into two scenes. *Les Ménechmes* opens with the Roman gods Apollo and Mercury lounging around Mt Parnassus discussing, among other things, contemporary French tastes in theatre; they invite Plautus to join them. Mercury asks the playwright whether he thinks today's Parisians would be interested in the kind of comedies that he wrote in ancient Rome. Plautus replies:

> I strongly doubt it. The characters,
> the spirits, the habits and the manners
> have changed so much in the past two thousand years, I believe.
> ...
> Unless Apollo were to choose a French author with a good sense for
>   comedy,
> who might overhaul everything at his whim;
> bring the play onto a new stage, change, build, and deconstruct
>   [*accommoder le tout à sa manière; porter la scène ailleurs, changer,*
>   *faire et défaire*].
> If he could succeed in this noble design,
> half French, half Roman [*Moitié Français, moitié romain*],
> then maybe I could still please the public.
>
>   Prologue.2.159-199[23]

Apollo recalls how he met an author recently, who showed him a play he was working on called *Les Ménechmes*, which he said was inspired by Plautus. Hearing this, the Roman playwright wholeheartedly endorses the project:

> Though I am the author, I bear no jealousy.
> Let's hope my opus will be useful to him.
> The topic he selected amused in the past
> a difficult audience. And maybe he will
> have the same outcome in Paris.
>
>   Prologue.2.205-9

To this, Mercury responds with his own benediction:

Under these happy auspices, I am going to arrange
right away all necessary things
to insure the play's success.

Prologue.2.210-12

Thus, the comedy begins with Plautus passing the torch to Regnard, and with Apollo and Mercury gesturing their approval. In this metatheatrical moment, Regnard underlines the play's literary pedigree and invokes heavenly support for its success. It is a bold – arguably hubristic – move on the playwright's part, but with it, he makes an impassioned case for his place in the classical tradition. With this programmatic prologue, Regnard sets out to 'overhaul everything ... change, build, and deconstruct' (*accommoder le tout à sa manière . . . changer, faire et défaire*, Prologue.2.96) in order to create his half-French, half-Roman hybrid (*Moitié Français, moitié romain*, Prologue.2.198). The first order of business is shifting the setting; he abandons the Graeco-Roman-Nowhere 'Plautinopolis' of Epidamnus and relocates the action to his hometown of Paris.

Act 1, Scene 1 opens with Le Chevalier Ménechme alone onstage, fuming at his valet Valentin, who is late to meet him. Valentin soon enters, likely running, certainly gasping for air. The stage directions explicitly indicate that he is carrying a suitcase, which he puts down and promptly sits upon:

Le Chevalier Where are you coming from, bad servant? Tell me, speak, answer!

Valentin Right now Monsieur I can't tell you;
One moment please, let me breathe
I am short of breath [*s'il vous plaît, souffrez que je respire/ Je suis tout essoufflé*]

Le Chevalier Do you want to throw me into despair every day?
I don't know how I hold myself from giving you twenty strikes with my cane ...
[*je ne sais qui me tient, que de vingt coups de canne . . .*].
You, rascal, how much time do you really need
To go to the customs office to get my suitcase?

1.2.243-250

We learn that Le Chevalier Ménechme's suitcase was lost during their travels, and that Valentin, who was supposed to pick it up forthwith from the customs office, instead spent much of the day drinking. He eventually recovers a suitcase with a tag addressed to 'Monsieur Ménechme, currently in Paris' (1.2.323). Le Chevalier Ménechme neither recognizes the suitcase nor is he able to open it with his key. Master and valet eventually break the suitcase open, only to discover unfamiliar rustic clothing along with a bundle of letters inside. A good deal sharper than his Plautine counterpart, Le Chevalier Ménechme reads one of the letters and immediately connects the dots. His subsequent dialogue with Valentin effectively serves the same function as Plautus' expository prologue:

> **Le Chevalier**   You know I was born near Peronne
> From a bloodline of no particular value.
> You know that having lost father and mother
> And being left penniless in my earliest years
> Tired of spending my time lost in the countryside
> I decided at fifteen to became a soldier.
> I left my twin brother in the house
> With an uncle avaricious and rich
> And I know by people who have told me
> That for many years my brother believes I am dead.
> **Valentin**   I know, also I know that your mother
> Died of childbirth of you and your brother
> That you are twins, and so identical
> That your looks and his are so similar
> That two drops of milk could not be so alike [*Que deux gouttes de
> lait ne sont pas plus semblables*]
>
> 1.2.368-385

From the letter, Le Chevalier Ménechme learns that the twins' uncle has died and that he has left a large sum of money to the Ménechme who lived with him in his house. Contingent upon his receiving the money is an arranged marriage with Mademoiselle Isabelle, daughter of a Parisian bourgeois named Demophon.

Le Chevalier Ménechme is thunderstruck. He quickly realizes that the suitcase belongs to his brother who is likely in Paris at that very moment. Furthermore, it turns out that *he* – Le Chevalier Ménechme – is in love with this very same Isabelle! But now there are two obstacles in the way of their love: (1) her apparent betrothal to his twin brother and (2) the fact that, in his penury, he is currently courting her wealthy aunt Araminte. Valentin succinctly sums up the spirit of the comedy when he says: 'I am amazed at the surprising effects that fate brings on' (*je suis stupéfait/ Des effets surprenants que le hasard a faits*, 1.2.410-411).

Unsure of how this will all play out, Le Chevalier Ménechme decides to hedge his bets and invest in his relationship with his affluent older patroness:

> **Le Chevalier**   I am going to Araminte; she knows I am back;
> I will have to pretend that I am dying of love.
> She has no idea that I have a new love interest.
> You know her character and her spirit:
> She is old and jealous;
> Her airs and her fashions are all dreadful;
> Well, she is crazy and wants to be flattered.
> Even though I am hoping that my new love will flourish,
> Uncertain of my success, I want to placate her.
>
> 1.2.430-40

Already in these preliminary scenes, then, Regnard makes good on his pledge to recreate the original Plautine comedy while simultaneously 'overhaul[ing] everything' (Prologue.2.196). He translates some of the dialogue verbatim from the Latin, for example at 1.2.385, when Valentin remarks that twins are so identical 'that two drops of milk could not be so alike' (*Que deux gouttes de lait ne sont pas plus semblables*). This line echoes *Menaechmi* 1088–1090 when Messenio finally sees the brothers side by side and makes the same observation.[24] While Plautus employs this analogy at the very end of his play, Regnard notably relocates it to the beginning, as if picking up where Plautus left off.

Regnard also draws from Plautus' pool of character types, while furnishing them with palpably new personalities. Like Messenio, Valentin is a loyal servant with an independent streak. He steps further out of line than his prototype, though, as evidenced by his day of drinking and his dubious scruples, thus departing from Messenio's paradigmatic 'Good Slave'. At the same time, Valentin is a Plautine *servus*; he is the mastermind behind – and an indispensable agent of – his master's madcap scheme and, in many ways, he is the heart and hero of the comedy.[25] He even performs the running slave routine! His aerobic exertions delay his very first words in the play: 'One moment please, let me breathe: I am short of breath' (*s'il vous plaît, souffrez que je respire/ Je suis tout essoufflé*, 1.2.245-6). Further reinforcing the New Comic master–slave dynamic, Le Chevalier Ménechme threatens him with conventional Plautine violence: 'I don't know how I hold myself from giving you twenty strikes with my cane' (*je ne sais qui me tient, que de vingt coups de canne*, 1.2.248).[26]

Le Chevalier Ménechme also has a good deal in common with his ancient counterpart. He too makes his grand entrance in a fit of fury, in this case complaining about Valentin rather than the *matrona*. A young man in love with a maiden, at first glance he seems to fit the mould of a traditional Plautine *adulescens*. At the same time, he also reveals himself to be an opportunistic flatterer who feigns affection in order to take advantage of a wealthy patron(ess). In this way, he more closely resembles both Peniculus the parasite *and* Erotium the prostitute than his correlative Menaechmus of Epidamnus. In fact, the most similar figure to Menaechmus E in *Les Ménechmes* is arguably Araminte, in the way that she both exploits her status over subordinate characters and embodies the comedic 'Pleasure Principle'.[27] She is also the comic converse of the *senex*; while they are likely around the same age (i.e. old enough to be the protagonists' parents), he derives comedy by leaning into his dotage, she by playing against it:

Araminte   At my age I might still hope to get married and to have children!

Demophon   Are you kidding, my sister? You are 50 years old!

Araminte   Me, 50 years old! Me! Finette?

...

Demophon   My sister in my calculation ...
I am 50 and some;
You are my elder, ergo in one word,
You see whether I am wrong.

Araminte   Your ergo is just an idiot; ...
What I can tell you in clear terms
Is that you will have to do without my monies;
That I feel better than all of you;
That despite all the plots you are building against me
I plan to bury, with God's help
The children I will have, you, and my niece ...

1.5.553-6; 560-71

Regnard thus 'deconstructs', 'changes', and '[re]builds' (Prologue.2.196) Plautus' cast here, adding new angles to his characters and new complications to his story.

Indeed, the story itself shifts its focus: no longer revolving around one brother's search for the other, the plot now rests on the premise that one twin knows *exactly* where his brother is, why he is there, and how he might exploit this knowledge for personal gain. It is Valentin, the cunning valet, who comes up with the plan: Le Chevalier Ménechme will dress up in his brother's clothes – conveniently packed in the mislaid suitcase – and pretend to be his twin. This way, he will not only inherit his uncle's fortune, but he will also get to marry fair young Isabelle instead of feisty old Araminte (2.1.621-39). If everything works out as it should, Valentin will also wed Finette, Araminte's clever maid and his female foil. In a rare moment of morality, Le Chevalier Ménechme pauses to grapple with the ethics of deceiving his brother (2.1.640). The cynical servant quickly disabuses him of his sentimentality:

Valentin   What vain and ridiculous sappiness!
Take everything you can; don't count on chance;
After, if you want, you can give him his share.

If he really cared about the money, who's to say
that he would show the same consideration for you.

2.1.641-5

Not long after Le Chevalier Ménechme agrees to the ruse, his twin brother, Ménechme, arrives in Paris. He immediately runs into Valentin and casually shares his life story with this stranger, who of course recognizes him as his master's twin. Valentin offers to be his valet and make all the arrangements for him during his stay in Paris.[28] In so doing, he can keep an eye on him and engineer the successful execution of his scheme. Ménechme gratefully, gullibly accepts. Luck would seem to be on both of their sides until Finette spots them and presses the wrong Ménechme to visit her mistress, his fiancée. In this way, Finette knocks over the first game piece in a long and spiralling domino row of mistaken identity bits involving each of the characters in mechanical turn.

It is not until the very last scene that the twin brothers meet face to face, finally in the same place at the same time, much to everyone's surprise and delight. A storybook happy ending, Le Chevalier Ménechme proposes that the twins split the inheritance, and Demophon allows his daughter to choose her own husband: 'You need a husband: here are two for one. Choose the good one for yourself, my daughter, and be content' (5.6.1891-2). Isabelle, of course, chooses her beloved Chevalier. His twin brother, Ménechme, then decides to marry Araminte, a practical choice for a practical man, and Valentin proposes to Finette. The curtain closes on the joyful celebration of three marriages.

While there are many clear and compelling points of contact between Regnard's *Les Ménechmes* and Plautus' *Menaechmi*, the two comedies also differ from one another in fundamental ways. Three 'modernizing' features of the eighteenth-century adaptation radically transpose the tone and takeaway of the ancient play: (1) a pair of actors playing the twins, (2) female actresses playing female roles, and (3) a relatively more homogenous and urbane primary audience.[29]

The original register receipts of the Comédie-Française all but conclusively prove that two actors played the titular twins in the original production.[30] While they helpfully list the names of all the performers, unfortunately, they do not specify the parts that each played. The Comédie-Française did not begin systematically recording this information until 1765. Casting registers after 1765, however, confirm that the size of the cast remained the same and that two different actors regularly played the Ménechme brothers from that point on.

However alike these two actors may have looked, they no longer had the advantage of sharing the same face or mask to render them truly identical. For this reason, Regnard decided to largely de-emphasize their physical resemblance and lean into their *dissimilarities*, especially with regard to their personalities. As Lucas (1843: 197) observes, the playwright gave the twins very different temperaments: Le Chevalier Ménechme is 'polite, gallant, and soft-spoken' (*poli, galant, doucereux*) while his brother Ménechme is 'brutal, brutish, and boorish' (*brutal, loup-garou, mauvais coucheur*). In this way, Regnard refocused the lens through which he wanted the audience to view the twins' (dis) connection with one another.

With regard to the female roles, by Regnard's time, women had already been acting on the French stage for about a hundred years.[31] In contrast to Plautus' *Matrona*, Ancilla, and Erotium, Regnard's Isabelle, Finette and Araminte were played by actual women, as opposed to cross-dressing men. In fact, because of the meticulous record-keeping of the Comédie-Française, we actually know the names of the actresses who performed in the original production on 4 December 1705: Mademoiselle Dangeville, Madame Desmares and Mademoiselle Des Brosses. While the precise roles that they played in *Les Ménechmes* were not noted, based on the types that the actresses tended to play in the troupe, it is likely that Mademoiselle Dangeville played the ingenue Isabelle, Madame Desmares played the *soubrette* Finette, and Mademoiselle Des Brosses renowned for her *caractère* roles, played Araminte.

Casting female actresses introduced new issues as well as new opportunities to the performance. On the one hand, like male actors in both Plautus' and Regnard's days, actresses in eighteenth-century France continued to bear some degree of social stigma (*infamia*), in their case, magnified all the more by religious moralism. As Berlanstein (1994: 475) notes, 'actresses occupied a contested place in eighteenth-century French society, and commentary about them sometimes evoked the very principles upon which the social order was based'. On the other hand, the realism that actresses brought to these roles in fact 'corrected' the transgression of transvestitism onstage and contributed to the comedy's broader sense of propriety. By this time, canon law actually forbade cross-dressing. Critics had to decide which was more sinful: seeing a woman on stage or seeing a man on stage pretending to be a woman.[32] For all the attendant *infamia*, however, theatre offered women a rare avenue for power. As star actresses became more and more famous, their name alone could draw audiences to a production. Most significantly, La Comédie-Française was – and continues to be – organized by members of its troupe. As *sociétaires de La Comédie-Française*, actresses have always had an equal say in production decisions as their male peers.

Finally, the audience played a dominant role in Regnard's reimagining of *Menaechmi*. While he could comfortably rely on the timeless appeal of the Mistaken Identity Bit, Regnard nonetheless had to adapt the story to suit contemporary styles and sensibilities. For this reason, he abandoned the central theme of adultery – at least among the humans and in the main part of the play (in the prologue, Apollo and Mercury casually gossip about the gods' extramarital affairs). Regnard purges his plot of this Plautine miasma. In his version, neither twin is married, and the prostitute has been decommissioned and disassembled, scraps of her personality repurposed in the construction of Le Chevalier Ménechme and Araminte. Her presence is still palpable, however, notably in the dinner scene where Araminte unwittingly wines and dines the wrong Ménechme (2.5), which maps neatly on to the parallel scene between Erotium and Menaechmus S at *Menaechmi* 351–445.

These revisions reveal a key difference between Plautus' and Regnard's audiences. Whereas Plautine comedies were performed at carnivalesque public festivals for diverse audiences (male and female, old and young, wealthy and poor, Roman and foreign, free, freed, and enslaved), Regnard's work targeted a more elite, educated, courtly audience. As Lancaster (1951: 594) notes, the audience of La Comédie-Française was 'probably composed largely of nobles, bourgeois, and artisans. The poorer members of society could not often afford the price of admission even to the *parterre*, though they came when there were free performances and were represented at other times by the lackeys and coachmen to whom Lesage refers as occupying the third tier of boxes'. At the illustrious home of the French National Theatre, context now called for more decorous content and characters.

The public greeted the play with enthusiasm. The critics applauded the vivacity of the verse, the fast pace of the action, and Regnard's skill in weaving an intricate plot and integrating the amusing confusion at every turn. Regnard, like Plautus, excelled at linguistical acrobatics and genuinely enjoyed regaling his audience with fun and puns. To commemorate the two hundredth anniversary of Regnard's death, a monument was inaugurated in his hometown of Dourdan on Sunday, 5 December 1909. A delegate from the venerable Academie Française in Paris delivered a speech which in many ways sums up the French comic playwright's creative and personal connection to his Roman model:

> Regnard is one of these masters who, in the large gallery of theater ancestors, faithfully kept alive the old traditions and the gift of joyful comedy and laughter … It is not the laughter of Terence, it is the laughter of Plautus, who Regnard admired and followed … Distance and Nature brought together Regnard, who had been beaten during his captivity in Algiers, and Plautus, the slave who laboriously pushed the grinding wheel in the bakery shop of his Roman master. And just like the Latin fellow, the good French man, despite all his misfortunes, kept laughing. Look at him, love him, and read him (*Et comme le Latin, le bon Français, malgré ses malheurs, continuait à rire. Regardez-le, aimez-le, et lisez-le …*).[33]

Carlo Goldoni, *The Venetian Twins (I Due Gemelli Veneziani)* (1748)

Like Shakespeare and Regnard before him, Goldoni was profoundly influenced by classical drama. With the spirit of Plautine comedy whispering in one ear and the spirit of *commedia dell'arte* whispering in the other, he developed the next major *riforma* in Italian theatre: Comedic Realism. Goldoni would explore this idea more fully in his 1750 play, *The Comic Theatre*, wherein he explicitly articulates his theatrical theories and reforms. Indeed, in his preface to *The Comic Theatre*, Goldoni (1969: 3) calls the play 'less a comedy in itself than a Foreword to all my Comedies.' It is in this play, *The Comic Theatre*, that Goldoni famously coins the term '*commedia dell'arte*', only to criticize it and then ultimately remake it. (Earlier terms used to describe the theatrical form include: *la commedia a soggetto* [situation comedy], *la commedia all'Italian* [Italian comedy], *commedia all'improvviso* [improvised comedy], and *comedia di zanni* [comedy of zanni]). Between *The Venetian Twins* and *The Comic Theatre*, Goldoni demonstrates and discusses a fundamental point about *commedia dell'arte*, namely that the form is ever changing, ebbing and flowing, dying and being reborn, moving to the classics and then away from them. Goldoni is simply the latest of its innovators. Interrogating the past, present and future of Italian comedy, he restored the orderliness of Plautus' tightly constructed plots to *commedia dell'arte's* elastic scenarios, he 'naturalized' their masked character types, and he breathed fresh life into their age-old forms and formulas.

Goldoni was born in Venice on 25 February 1707. He fell in love with theatre at a young age reading comedies in his father's library. By his own admission, however, he was a terrible student. In his memoirs, Goldoni (1926: 14–15) confesses:

> I went very unwillingly: this professor, who was a man of great celebrity, wearied me dreadfully ... I wrote from his dictation; but, instead of going over my note-books at home, I nourished my mind with a much

more useful and agreeable philosophy; I read Plautus, Terence, Aristophanes, and the fragments of Menander.

He was so apathetic towards his formal education – and so passionate about theatre – that he even ran away from school with a travelling troupe of actors at the age of fourteen. He later attended the Ghislieri College in Pavia where he studied, among other subjects, French in order to read Molière's work in its original language. He had already begun writing plays by this time. His collegiate experience was abruptly cut short in 1725, when he was expelled for writing a particularly provocative Atellan farce. While Goldoni himself refers to it as an 'Atellano', its precise connection to the ancient genre remains unclear, beyond a shared sense of ribaldry. The piece, entitled *The Colossus (Il Colosso)*, imagined an enormous statue that indiscreetly combined some prominent physical features of some prominent Pavian ladies. Their respectable – and powerful – families did not find it funny:

> The Atellano became the novelty of the day, and those who were not implicated in it, laughed at the work, while they condemned the author. Twelve families cried for vengeance, and my life was sought after; but fortunately for me, I was still under arrest.
>
> Goldoni [1926: 52]

Though Goldoni escaped more severe punishment through the intervention of well-placed protectors, he was forced to leave Pavia. Writing about the episode some sixty years later, the playwright reflects on it with a combination of contrition and puckish pride.

Goldoni fared better studying at Udine, and he later received his law degree from the University of Modena. He went on to practice law in both Venice (1731–3) and Pisa (1744–8), where he also served a number of diplomatic positions. Still, his heart belonged to the theatre. In Pisa, he was visited by an up-and-coming comedic actor by the name of Cesare D'Arbes, who requested that Goldoni write a play for him. After a moment's deliberation (and a glance into the box of money that D'Arbes had proffered), the playwright accepted the invitation. He then inquired whether the actor wished to play his role masked or unmasked.

Up to that point, D'Arbes had never performed without a mask; this would be his ideal opportunity to do so. Goldoni wrote the piece, *The Elegant Antonio* (*Tonin Belia Gratia*), for D'Arbes in three weeks. Resigning from his law practice to focus on theatre full-time, Goldoni returned to Venice in 1748 for the production of *The Elegant Antonio.* Chatfield-Taylor (1913: 181) observes, 'No longer a dilettante, nor a briefless lawyer, no longer a young vagabond inspired by *wanderlust*, he was a man past forty, who to earn his bread had articled himself to an exacting manager, his task being to furnish dramatic material of a nature sufficiently popular to make the operation of a theatre profitable.' Fortified by his apparent good fortune and gratifying career-change, Goldoni was pleased with the script he had written and heartened by the actors' laughter during rehearsals. It seemed like the stars were aligning for a smash hit. Unfortunately, the audiences didn't agree. *The Elegant Antonio* turned out to be a spectacular flop. In his memoirs, Goldoni (1926: 239) laments:

> I shall only observe, in atonement for my fault, that when I wrote this comedy, I had been four years out of practice; my head was occupied with my professional employment; I was uneasy in my mind, and in bad humour, and, to add to my misfortune, it was approved of by my actors. We were sharers in the folly, and we were equal sharers in the loss.

To console the humiliated D'Arbes, Goldoni immediately began working on two projects for his lead actor. The first would be an 'easy' play, which the comedian could perform in a mask: *The Prudent Man* (*L'Uomo Prudente*). The second, would be a more challenging star vehicle, to be performed without a mask. It would become one of Goldoni's greatest masterpieces: *The Venetian Twins (I Due Gemelli Veneziani).*

The Prudent Man was very well received in Venice. Wearing a mask and playing his acclaimed Pantalone role, the lead actor was securely in his comfort zone. It gave him the opportunity to rebuild his confidence as well as his reputation. Goldoni (1926: 239) remarks, 'Darbes [*sic*] could not possibly have been more at his ease in displaying the superiority of his talents in the different shades which he had to express. Nothing more was necessary to procure him the general character of the most accomplished actor then on the stage.' Studying D'Arbes closely during the run of *The Prudent Man*, Goldoni devoted himself to the careful composition of *The Venetian Twins*. He developed the title characters with his lead actor in mind:

> I had had sufficient time and opportunities to examine into the different personal characters of my actors. In Darbes [*sic*] I perceived two opposite and habitual movements in his figure and his actions. At one time, he was the gayest, the most brilliant and lively man in the world; and at another, he assumed the air, the manners, and conversation of a simpleton and a blockhead. These changes took place quite naturally and without reflection.
>
> This discovery suggested to me the idea of making him appear under these different aspects in the same play.
>
> Goldoni [1926: 239]

Thus D'Arbes inspired the double role of Zanetto (the uncouth twin) and Tonino (the debonair twin). The success of Goldoni and D'Arbes' subsequent collaborations far eclipsed the failure of their first project together. *The Venetian Twins*, in particular, gave D'Arbes a chance to both save face and truly show his face for all to see:

> The play was extolled to the very skies. The incomparable acting of Darbes [*sic*] contributed infinitely to its success. His glory and his joy were at their height. The director was not less pleased to witness the complete success of his undertaking, and I had my share also in the general satisfaction in seeing myself caressed and applauded a great deal more than I deserved.
>
> Goldoni [1926: 239–40]

Between his return to Venice in 1748 and his departure in 1762, Goldoni wrote almost two hundred plays. He moved to Paris in 1762 to direct the Comédie-Italienne; he remained there for two years before accepting a position teaching Italian to the French princesses at

Versailles. He began writing his memoirs – in French – at the age of eighty in 1783. Despite his venerable status and accomplishments, he died in poverty, having lost his pension during the French Revolution, on 6 February 1793 in Paris at the age of eighty-six.

Let us take closer look now at this game-changing play, which would cement Goldoni's reputation as one of the preeminent comedic writers of his time and herald the next major phase of Italian theatre. *The Venetian Twins* is about a pair of physically identical, ethically antithetical brothers, who are unaware that they are in the same place at the same time, and cause all sorts of complications for one another and for the characters in their orbit. The plot encompasses a series of errant love stories sent spinning out in every direction by the centrifugal forces of greed, passion and, of course, mistaken identity. Zanetto, the boorish but wealthy brother, has come to Verona to marry Rosaura the daughter of Doctor Balanzoni. Meeting her future husband for the first time, Rosaura is appalled by his ignorance and incivility, but as a dutiful daughter, she tries to honour her father's wishes nonetheless. Tonino, the gracious and humble brother, is also in town to wed. Planning to elope with his beloved Beatrice, he had to depart from their hometown of Venice separately from her. They arranged to meet and marry in Verona. Tonino asked his dear friend Florindo to accompany Beatrice on the journey, and also to call him by his brother's name, Zanetto, in order to protect his identity. Upon his arrival in Verona, Tonino finds Florindo . . . but not Beatrice. Family secrets, rival lovers, and plain old confusion threaten the unions – and reunion – of the brothers.

The story takes place in Verona, at once a declaratively *Italian* location and, at the same time, worlds away from Venice, Goldoni's own hometown and the venue of the comedy's first production. As in Plautus and Shakespeare, the Familiar-Yet-Foreign setting allows Goldoni to play with the sense of distance between his characters and his audience. Unlike the brothers in *Menaechmi* and *The Comedy of Errors*, both Venetian Twins are travellers here; neither lives in the city where the play is set and so both navigate the space with an outsider's perspective. Tonino, the righteous twin, embodies Venetian virtues. He is an honest and honourable figure, and he frequently draws connections between his city and his values (e.g. 'When you insult my friend you insult me. In Venice we value friendship above life. I would disgrace the city of my birth if I did not defend him' (Bolt [1993: 23]).[34] Zanetto, on the other hand, the coarse country-bumpkin, identifies exclusively with Bergamo where he now lives. When the chief constable explains the bureaucratic hoops through which he would have to jump to reclaim his lost jewels, Zanetto announces that he'd rather go home to the countryside without them than deal with these corrupt and overly complicated city-systems: 'Ta very much! I'm off back to my hills. There are no judges there – no lawyers, no guards. There, what's yours is yours, and you don't go bankrupt trying to get justice' (Bolt [1993: 72]). Verona, then, stands in for a generic *purgatorio* relative to both twins' versions of *paradiso*.

Even with its eighteenth-century Venetian mien and manners, Goldoni's play is an ancient Roman Comedy at heart. Structurally, it resembles *Menaechmi* in its clockwork progression of the action. While the play has been condensed into three acts, it continues to balance each brother's storyline more or less evenly, despite the introduction of a new sibling (a long-lost sister!) to the mix. With tidy symmetry, Goldoni bookends the play with her; he plants the seeds for her appearance in the very first scene and formally recognizes her at the conclusion of the story. The play achieves elegant equilibrium on a scene-to-scene scale as well, for example, the transition between 3.15 and 3.16, where one scene ends with Rosaura ripping up a letter and throwing the pieces at Tonino, and the next one begins with Beatrice repeating the same routine.

While the plot no longer revolves around one brother's quest to find the other, the 'lost child' storyline remains central to the play's major revelation and resolution. Most significantly, the Mistaken Identicals theme continues to drive the momentum of the play and account for much of its comedy. With regard to *The Venetian Twins'* cast of characters, Goldoni borrows from Plautus by way of *commedia dell'arte*. Menaechmus E's impropriety, Peniculus' dishonesty and Erotium's eroticism are all present, just transfigured here. Zanetto inherits

Menaechmus E's amorous amorality; Pancrazio takes on Peniculus' self-serving duplicity, and even the pure and proper Rosaura finds herself in the position of an (accidental) prostitute when Tonino misreads her invitation to pay her a visit.

The characters are further filtered through the framework of *commedia dell'arte.* Columbina, Brighella and Arlecchino, for example, are all established servants (*zanni*) in the *commedia* tradition. Brighella, like Messenio, is a Good servant, who may in fact know more than she lets on, and who helps the hero work out the mystery. Columbina, on the other hand, more closely resembles Plautus' sassy *ancilla.* She routinely talks back to – and behind the back of! – her mistress Rosaura:

> **Columbina** (*Aside*)   Knowing my luck she'll turn out to be a lady.
> (*Aloud*) If she's someone important, please don't tell her I called her all those names.
> **Toninino**   Don't worry. I know maids – always maligning their mistresses (*Goes*).

Bolt [1993: 86]

Similarly, Arlecchino has a cheeky relationship with his 'master' Zanetto. When he first spots him at 2.1, he prepares to play a trick on him:

> **Arlecchino**   Ta very much. Here he comes now! Let's hide. I wants to play a trick on him. Just you see if he recognizes me.
> **Porter**   You shouldn't play tricks on your master.
> **Arlecchino**   Nay, we's pals, him and me.

Bolt [1993: 37]

Their friendship is tested, however, when Zanetto accuses him of stealing his money and jewels. Arlecchino in fact just gave them to the wrong twin. When Zanetto refuses to stand by him and allows the servant to be taken away and locked up, Arlecchino curses his former master. Their bond irreparably broken, he joins the growing list of people with ominous enmity toward Zanetto.

As in *Menaechmi,* misogyny continues to be a dominant, problematic theme of the comedy. The two ingenues are almost 'tragic' figures, hyperbolically sober and serious. Beatrice lives only for Tonino, and threatens to kill herself on more than one occasion, if she can't belong to him and him alone. Rosaura obediently submits to her father's authority again and again (even after discovering his dishonourable motives for marrying her off . . . and the fact that that he is not her real father!). On the one hand, these women derive power by embodying the play's moral compass. At the same time, neither of them has any real autonomy or identity apart from the men who objectify and transact them. They are instruments of the comedy's happy ending, but not unequivocal beneficiaries of it. Beatrice and Tonino have a lot of unresolved issues to work out and Rosaura isn't exactly exultant to marry the buffoon Lelio.

Marriage itself is once again the subject of satire in this play. When Pancrazio tries to dissuade Zanetto from marrying Rosaura, his words echo the negative matrimonial messaging in *Menaechmi*:

Pancrazio Marriage is a chain that holds a husband like a slave to a galley.

Zanetto Marriage?

Pancrazio Yes, marriage.

Zanetto What a load of old rubbish!

Pancrazio Marriage is a burden that makes you sweat by day and keeps you awake at night. It is a burden on the mind and on the body. And worst of all, it empties the purse.

Zanetto You don't say! That's terrible!

Pancrazio And the woman who seems to beautiful at first – so gentle – what do you think she really is?

Zanetto Tell me. Tell me.

Pancrazio A siren who will lure you to your destruction. Who will flatter you to deceive and plunge you into penury . . .

Zanetto God bless thee!

Pancrazio Women. . .?

Zanetto Uhgggh!

Pancrazio Marriage?

Zanetto Ahgggh!

Pancrazio Never again?

Zanetto Never again.

Pancrazio   Certain?
Zanetto   Abso-bloody-lutely!

Bolt [1993: 31–2]

Pancrazio's criticism here is counterbalanced to some extent by Tonino's defence of a good marriage and a good woman:

> Rubbish! A burden on the mind? On the contrary, a wife can relieve your anxiety. She looks after the finances and the servants. With that natural feminine cunning, which some people call avarice, she may even – at the end of the year – make profits for the household. You know what the Venetian poet says: 'You'll marry if you've got a brain and aren't averse to compromise. Those who oppose what I advise are impotent or else insane.'

Bolt [1993: 57]

While it doesn't erase the play's misogyny, at the very least, this speech introduces an alternate perspective and begins to steer the conversation in a new direction from *Menaechmi*.

Stylistically, *The Venetian Twins* has a great deal in common with *Menaechmi*, especially in its deployment of word play, physical comedy, and even its farcical use of talismans (i.e. the box of jewels). One of the most striking stylistic similarities between the two comedies, however, is their exercise of metatheatre. Like *Menaechmi*, *The Venetian Twins* regularly recognizes and exploits its status as a play, notably through the use of asides. Just about every character turns to the audience at one point or another and uses the device to reveal their secrets, their intentions, and/or their true natures to the audience. When Tonino finally solves the mystery and grasps the fact that Rosaura is his long-lost sister, Flaminia, he shares this revelation first and foremost with the audience in an aside. By this point, asides are such a standard feature of the dialogue that they effectively 'go without saying'. Seizing this golden opportunity for a metatheatrical joke, however, Columbina immediately delivers her own aside to the audience, pointing out how absurd and unrealistic this convention is: 'Why's he talking to himself?' (Bolt [1993: 85]). Fully committing to this line of metatheatrical humour, Tonino announces (in another aside): 'She's definitely my sister. What a happy coincidence! Two brothers and a sister – all here – together! It's like something in a comedy' (Bolt [1993: 85]).

While Goldoni generally followed Plautus' comedic recipe, mixing many of *Menaechmi*'s ingredients – both salty and sweet – into the Italian sausage that is *The Venetian Twins*, he also adjusted the seasonings to suit contemporary tastes. His two most significant innovations to the Plautine original are arguably: (1) the casting of a single *unmasked* actor to play both twins and (2) the shocking decision to end the comedy with not just one, but two deaths. In addition to taking the play in an entirely new and unexpected direction, these choices also had a significant impact on the future of Italian drama.

Thanks to Goldoni's own memoirs, we know for a fact that he wrote the dual roles of the titular twins for one actor, Cesare D'Arbes. The success of the play, then, effectively hinged on its star's virtuosity and the production's ability to exploit the dramatic illusion of the doubles to the fullest. Since Goldoni deliberately chose to abandon the use of masks – a long-standing convention of both ancient Roman drama and contemporary *commedia dell'arte* – appearances took on all new meaning. Characters often call attention to – and judge one another by – their looks, for example, when Rosaura first meets Zanetto ('Not bad looking. Perhaps he's not as stupid as Brighella made out' [Bolt (1993: 12)] or when she sees Pancrazio coming ('You can tell from his face what a good man he is' (Bolt [1993: 16]). The snappiest illustration of this is arguably 2.6, when Columbina sees her future husband, Arlecchino for the first time:

Columbina	What a handsome man!
Arlecchino	I'll ask that comely wench if she's seen him.
Arlecchino	D'you know tis Signora Rosaura?
Columbina	Very well.
Arlecchino	And her maid. . .?
Columbina	I am her maid.
Arlecchino	You!
Columbina	Me.

Arlecchino	Dost tha know who I am?
Columbina	No.
Arlecchino	Only Arlecchino Battocchio.
Columbina	You? Arlecchino Battocchio?
Arlecchino	Ay! That's right!
Columbina	My husband!
Arlecchino	My bride!
Columbina	You're handsome!
Arlecchino	You're a smasher!
Columbina	What bliss!
Arlecchino (*Aside*)	What a relief!

Bolt [1993: 44–5]

Since the twins were now physically indistinguishable from one another (i.e. conspicuously played by one and the same actor), D'Arbes would have to transform both his voice and his body language in order to differentiate between the two roles. His interlocutors regularly comment on how his voice seems to change. Indeed, Rosaura even wonders if there's more to it than that: 'I'd like you to explain one thing. You seem to be two different people – sometimes stupid, sometimes intelligent – sometimes forward, sometimes shy. What does it all mean?' (Bolt [1993: 79]). What a star role for a capable actor!

Goldoni's decision to suspend the use of masks was a radical one, and it met with conservative criticism, especially by rival playwrights like Pietro Chiari and Carlo Gozzi. Goldoni (1926: 300) defends his position in his memoirs by condemning *commedia dell'arte* for its lack of a clear, polished Italian voice and form, as well as for its obsolete – indeed, disadvantageous – use of masks:

> The masks of the Greeks and Romans were a sort of speaking trumpets, invented for the purpose of conveying the sound through the vast extent of their amphitheatres. Passion and sentiment were not, in those times, carried to the pitch of delicacy now actually necessary. The actor must, in our days, possess a soul; and the soul under a mask is like a fire under ashes. These were the reasons which induced me to endeavor the reform of the Italian theatre, and to supply the place of farces with comedies.

The Venetian Twins proved that these innovations enabled 'classic' Italian comedy not only to survive, but indeed to thrive. As Davies (1968: 21) notes, '*The Venetian Twins* ... was the first play in which *commedia dell'arte* actors went on the stage without their masks and triumphed. With this play the most fickle and yet most conservative audience in Italy gave its consent to the final disappearance of the old Comedy of Masks and to the build-up by Goldoni of a national comedy.'

So how did Goldoni solve the problem of the twins meeting face to face at the end of the play? Simple: he killed one off. Goldoni begins laying the groundwork for this early on by giving several characters motives to murder Zanetto, notably Lelio, Florindo, Arlecchino and Pancrazio. As the plot accelerates towards the denouement, it becomes more and more apparent that it's no longer a question of *when*, but rather *who* will actually kill him. Pancrazio is the ultimate culprit, poisoning Zanetto in act of desperate jealousy with the jewellery-cleaning powder he had picked up earlier in the play. What is more, Pancrazio drinks the rest of the poison himself, and so the play in fact ends with his suicide. While these are convenient dramatic solutions, they are also deeply unsettling. Comedies don't end with murder/suicides, do they? Goldoni clearly wanted to shake things up and prove that comedies of errors don't have to be predictable in order to be successful. He understood, however, that the deaths needed to be appropriately 'comical'. In his prefatory notes to the play, Goldoni muses:

> [Zanetto's death] does not bring any sadness to the audience, but rather amuses them because of the ridiculous nonsense with which the poor fool dies [*in questa mia non reca all'uditore tristezza alcuna; ma lo diverte per la sciocchezza ridicola con cui va morendo il povero sventurato*][35]

The shock of seeing the dead Zanetto carried offstage is, in fact, a brilliant set-up for the surprise of seeing the very-much-alive Tonino (re)appear a split second later from the opposite wing. The tragedy of the character's death, then, heightens the comedy of the actor's 'resurrection'. By blending theatricality and realism, Goldoni simultaneously rewrote the ending of *Menaechmi* and the rules of Italian drama.

Richard Rodgers (music), Lorenz Hart (lyrics), and George Abbott (book), *The Boys From Syracuse* (1938)

The twins' voyage from Syracuse to Manhattan took a long time, approximately twenty-three centuries and 4,583 miles over the Atlantic Ocean. Inspiration for *The Boys From Syracuse* fortuitously struck Richard Rodgers and Lorenz Hart as they set out to write an entirely different play. The famous friends, collaborators and composers of American musical theatre were on a train to Atlantic City to begin working on *I Married an Angel*, when they found themselves discussing the striking resemblance between Hart's younger brother Teddy, a rising comedian, and Jimmy Savo, a popular comedic actor of the day. Imagine the hilarity that might ensue from having these two funnymen play opposite one another! According to a cover story on Rodgers and Hart in *Time Magazine* published two months before *The Boys From Syracuse*'s 23 November 1938 premiere, 'they hit on the idea of putting Shakespeare to music, decided to swipe his *Comedy of Errors* ... which Shakespeare himself swiped from the *Menaechmi* of Plautus (who in turn swiped it from parties unknown)'. They reached out to their friend and fellow dramatist, George Abbott, to ask for his help. Abbott was so enthusiastic about the project that he immediately signed on to produce, direct and write the whole script. Upon reading his work, Rodgers said, 'the book was so sharp, witty, fast-moving and, in an odd way, so very much in keeping with the bawdy Shakespearean tradition that neither Larry nor I wanted to change a line'.[36]

The Boys From Syracuse reimagines Plautus' *Menaechmi* through the undisguised vehicle of Shakespeare's *The Comedy of Errors*. It opens with a comically brief prologue wherein Dromio of Syracuse and Dromio of Ephesus deliver these programmatic lines:

Dromio S. (*Stamps both feet in military fashion.*)   This is a drama of
     Ancient Greece.
Dromio E. (*Stamps.*)   It is a story of mistaken identity.
Dromio S. and **Dromio E.** (*Both stamp.*)   If it's good enough for
     Shakespeare, it's good enough for us.

                              Rodgers, Hart and Abbott [1965: 1][37]

With this blunt proclamation, the twentieth-century American
dramatists draw a bold, indelible, king-size Sharpie-marker line
connecting the dots between Plautus, Shakespeare and themselves. In
many ways, this tells the audience all they really need to know: the story
is set in the Greek(ish) world, it's about mistaken identity, and, hey, the
gimmick worked for Shakespeare so why not us? An 'easy' joke, it also
legitimizes the dramatists' larger theatrical project here and invests it
with comedic credibility.

     The Boys From Syracuse clearly – if loosely – follows the principal
plot points and main movements of *The Comedy of Errors* and, by
extension, *Menaechmi*. Condensing the lively dialogue, songs and dance
numbers into two acts, the modern American musical nonetheless
retains the basic horological structure of its sixteenth-century English
and ancient Roman models. Like Shakespeare – and likely Plautus –
before them, however, Rodgers, Hart and Abbott also took a number of
creative liberties with their source material, notably with the slave
character(s). Shakespeare, of course, added a second (twin) slave to
Plautus' comedy; Rodgers, Hart and Abbott preserved this modification,
but tweaked the slaves' backstory. In this new version, Antipholus of
Syracuse and Dromio of Syracuse are *both* looking for their long-lost
twins after arriving in Ephesus, whereas in Shakespeare's play, none of
the characters know that either Dromio has a brother until the very last
scene. This subtle change in fact goes a long way towards recalibrating
the balance of the story and shifting the focus more purposefully
toward the slaves. It also makes the title all the more ambiguous: who
exactly are the 'Boys from Syracuse'? Antipholus of Syracuse and
Dromio of Syracuse? The two Antipholus brothers? The two Dromio
brothers? All four of them? No longer mere side-kicks, the Dromios

become more central to the 'search story' than ever before. I would argue that this revision casts an even brighter spotlight on the leading roles of the double Dromios and further underscores the musical's *raison d'être*, namely to showcase the physical resemblance – and comedic talents – of Teddy Hart and Jimmy Savo, who played the 'identical' slaves (despite the fact that Jimmy Savo was a good 8 inches taller than Teddy Hart). Of note, while the four leading roles were expressly written for four different actors, the 1940 film adaptation of *The Boys From Syracuse* decided to double-cast the twins, with Allan Jones playing both Antipholi and Joe Penner playing both Dromios.

Simultaneously reflecting and refracting the setting of *The Comedy of Errors*, *The Boys From Syracuse* brings us back to good old Ephesus, only this time, the city is rendered even less multi-dimensional than before and more like a cardboard-cutout, slapdash-painted, hyperbolically 'Ancient' façade. Gone is the Abbess and her priory; in their place is a Seeress and her temple. Geographically, temporally and culturally, New York in the 1930s was even farther removed from ancient Ephesus than Stratford in the 1500s or Rome in the third/ second century BCE. Consequently, the concept of Ephesus comes across as more abstract and foreign than ever before. Despite this sense of distance – or perhaps *because* of it – Rodgers, Hart and Abbott, exploit this 'Plautinopolis' in much the same way as their predecessors did. A clear example of this can be seen in the song, 'Dear Old Syracuse':

> This is a terrible city.
> The people are cattle and swine.
> There isn't a girl I'd call pretty
> Nor a friend that I'd call mine.
> And the only decent place on earth
> Is the town that gave me birth.
>
> ... Wives don't want divorces there –
> The men are strong as horses there;
> And should a man philander
> The goose forgives the gander,

When the search for love becomes a mania
You can take the night boat to Albania.
I want to go back – go back –
To dear old Syracuse!

Rodgers, Hart and Abbott [1965: 8–9]

A modest, easily forgettable ballad, 'Dear Old Syracuse' is in fact doing a number of clever and functional things here: (1) it transports the audience from Broadway to the Ancient Mediterranean, (2) it makes learned allusions to notable Plautine and Shakespearean locales, (3) it underlines the dissonance between Syracuse and Ephesus, a central plot point, and most importantly, (4) its language blends and bends the boundaries between the classical and contemporary worlds. Like Plautus and Shakespeare before him, Hart wove his own time and place into his lyrics. The 'night boat to Albania', for example, is a thinly veiled reference to an infamous vessel that travelled back and forth between Manhattan and Albany along the Hudson River, departing 42nd Street around 8.00 pm in the evening and returning around 8.00 am the next day. A kind of floating motel, it was a notorious venue for illicit and scandalous affairs.[38] Like Plautus winking to his audience about the hassles of the Roman patronage system or Shakespeare raising a supercilious eyebrow at the similarities between Elizabethan slavery and servitude, here Rodgers, Hart and Abbott cast a knowing side-eye at the licentiousness of 1930s New York by way of dear old Syracuse.

The characters all bear a striking family resemblance to their theatrical ancestors. Like Shakespeare and Plautus' *adulescentes*, the modern Antipholus brothers fit familiar moulds: the local twin continues to be a philanderer, who puckishly personifies the Saturnalian spirit of comedy, while the travelling twin is serious and honourable (at least, relatively speaking). The newest Dromios on the block are closely modelled on Shakespeare's slaves of the same name, while also incorporating aspects of Plautus' Messenio and Peniculus. In Act 1, Scene 1, for example, when Antipholus of Ephesus refuses to go home to his wife, Dromio of Ephesus replies: 'Yeah. That's easy for you to say. But what about me? If you aren't home in time for dinner. She's gonna raise hell. I'll be the one that catches it …' (Rodgers, Hart and Abbott [1965: 4]). These lines evocatively echo Peniculus' words at 125–126: 'He may think he's bad-mouthing his wife, but I'm the one taking it in the jaw. If he dines out, he punishes my stomach, not his wife.' Though the Dromios take on some of Peniculus' parasitic features, they expressly personify the comedic *servus*. Together, they perform many of this stock character's 'greatest hits', including:

(1) Getting involved in his master's mischief:

> **Luce**   You're out curring up some high jinx with your master when you ought to be home giving me some attention. I need a lot of attention.
> **Dromio E.**   Well I do the best I can.
>
> Rodgers, Hart and Abbott [1965: 11]

(2) Stage violence:

> **Dromio E.**   If I come near him he'll beat me.
> **Adriana**   I'll beat you if you don't
> **Dromio E.** (*Backing to door R.*)   He kicks me to here and then you kick me back again. Boy, you sure get a kick out of me.
>
> Rodgers, Hart and Abbott [1965: 15]

And, of course, (3) the 'Running Slave Bit':

> **Dromio S.**   I'm exhausted. It was worse than the marathon (*X back to couch.*) I ran all the way.
>
> Rodgers, Hart and Abbott [1965: 49]

Interestingly enough, it is the women in *The Boys From Syracuse* who undergo the greatest metamorphoses from one adaptation to the next. They are still products of a misogynistic stereotypical tradition, but those stereotypes continue to evolve from play to play and cultural context to cultural context. By mixing and matching their traditional 'stock' characteristics with contemporary stylings, Rodgers, Hart and Abbott simultaneously reincarnate and reinvent Plautus' female figures. To illustrate this, let us take a closer look at the roles of the wife (*matrona*) and the prostitute (*meretrix*) in more detail.

As in *The Comedy of Errors*, the *matrona*'s role is much more complex – and personable – here than it is in *Menaechmi*. No longer anonymous, she retains the name that Shakespeare finally gave her: Adriana. And yet, Adriana is not the only wife in either *The Comedy of Errors* or *The Boys From Syracuse*. While she's married to the main *adulescens*, Luce and Emilia are technically wives as well. With their distinctive personalities and agendas, they add new dimensions to this *dramatis persona*. Together, these three characters expand the *matrona*'s range to include: sympathetic victim, comically insatiable lover, and loving life-partner and mother. At the same time, Plautus' battle-axe *matrona* is not entirely erased from the picture. In fact, the one direct quote that Abbott decided to keep from *The Comedy of Errors* speaks precisely to her character. In order to make absolutely sure that the audience catches the reference – and perhaps also to lighten the mood – Dromio of Syracuse pops out from behind the scenes like a living footnote:

Seeress   You should have reprimanded him.
Adriana   Oh, lady, I did. I never let up on him. In bed, he couldn't
   sleep for me scolding him. At table, I hardly let him eat for crying
   about his morals.
Seeress   What a wonderful system.
Adriana   Is it?
Seeress   For your rivals.
Adriana   What do you mean?
Seeress   The venom clamor of a jealous woman poisons more deadly
   than a mad dog's tooth.
Dromio S. (*Sticking head out of door of temple*): Shakespeare!
                    Rodgers, Hart and Abbott [1965: 56–7]

Likewise, the *meretrix*'s role continues to change. As in *The Comedy of Errors*, she is simply referred to as The Courtesan here, and, in a striking role reversal with the *matrona*, *she* becomes the play's main blocking figure. As the object of extramarital lust, she stands in the way of the comedy's new *telos*: true love between husband and wife. Even the adulterous Antipholus of Ephesus recognizes this: 'Yes, you've got something all right, but when it comes to *real* love, then a fellow has to turn to his wife' (Rodgers, Hart and Abbott [1965: 21]). Cue the love song: 'The Shortest Day of The Year'. Indeed, the chaste, but pregnant romance between Antipholus of Syracuse and Luciana, Adriana's sister, is the most idealized relationship in the play. With her sense of propriety and honourable restraint, Luciana contributes the character of the maiden (*virgo*) to the chorus of women.

On the one hand, in contrast to the *matrona* and the *virgo*, the *meretrix* and her methods are condemned as immoral. On the other hand, the men of Ephesus continue to lust after her and her fellow courtesans like comic satyrs. This kind of ludic 'mixed-messaging' continues to be as effective here as it was on the ancient comedic stage. Further complicating the ethical rubric of this story is the fact that Adriana, Luciana and Luce not only advocate, but literally sing the praises of the courtesan's techniques. The song, 'Sing For Your Supper', is one of the most famous and successful musical numbers to come from this show:

> **Adriana**   I'll tell you something right now, girls. You might imagine that you'll be lovebirds forever, but, it'll turn out to be different. But if you want a happy nest, you'll try to please them.
>
> Hawks and crows do lots of things
> But the canary only sings.
> She's a courtesan on wings –
> So I've heard.
> Eagles and storks are twice as strong,
> All the canary knows is song,
> But the canary gets along –
> Gilded bird!
>
> Sing for your supper
> And you'll get breakfast;
> Songbirds always eat
> If their song is sweet to hear.
> Sing for your luncheon
> And you'll get dinner!
> Dine with wine of choice

If romance is in your voice.
I heard from a wise canary
Trilling makes a fellow willing,
So, little swallow, swallow now.
Now is the time to
Sing for your supper
And you'll get breakfast.
Songbirds are not dumb.
They don't buy a crumb of bread,
It's said,
So sing and you'll be fed.

Rodgers, Hart and Abbott [1965: 46][39]

A playful ditty with a memorable hook, 'Sing For Your Supper' brings the ancient voices of the *parasitus*, the *meretrix*, the *matrona*, the *virgo* and the *ancilla* into modern harmony with one another.

Taken together, these characters reveal what is arguably the most dramatic transformation from *Menaechmi* to *The Comedy of Errors* to *The Boys From Syracuse*: the generic expansion from pure farcical comedy to romance.[40] While the 'search story' continues to propel the plot forward and the Mistaken Identity Bit continues to combust its comedy, the theme of love occupies a new, more centralized place in the play than ever before. It is the subject of no less than seven musical numbers. As Nolan (1995: 253) notes:

The score of *The Boys From Syracuse* is a delight; 'Falling In Love With Love' – with a whirling waltz melody that is said to have been Hart's favorite – is one of Rodgers and Hart's most elegantly bittersweet creations, while 'This Can't Be Love' demonstrates yet again Larry Hart's impeccable gift for the throwaway love song. The specialty numbers 'What Can You Do With A Man?' (introduced by Teddy Hart and outsize Wynn Murray – 'acres and acres of beauty going to waste') – and 'He and She' (Murray and Jimmy Savo), the story of a married couple so perfectly awful that when they died and went to Heaven all the angels moved to Hell, were witty and apposite.

While the score largely celebrates starry-eyed romantic love, it also delights in bursting that bubble and poking fun at love's less glamourous, more mundane aspects. In numbers like 'What Can You Do With A Man?', 'He and She' and 'Oh Diogenes', the women are given a platform to satirize the men and respond to the heavily misogynistic tradition of which they are a part. To be clear: neither *The Comedy of Errors* nor *The Boys From Syracuse* is presenting an unequivocally positive depiction of women or men. They are, however, in their own small ways, levelling the playing field a bit further by painting more equitably flawed and ridiculous portraits of both sexes.

Conclusion

Either directly or through its descendants, *Menaechmi* has reached more people in more forms than Plautus could ever have imagined. From European stages to American television, from Japanese manga to Bollywood and Nollywood cinema, the Mistaken Identicals motif has entertained – and continues to entertain – diverse audiences across diverse media across the centuries. Its timeless themes of Identity, Fortune, Love and Freedom are as relevant and meaningful today as they were in the third century BCE and its characters, while 'stock', are also accessibly, relatably, universally human. Like its titular twins, the play is at once silly and serious, familiar and foreign, simple and artful, and above all, eternal.

Appendix

Texts, translations and commentaries

Plautus' *Menaechmi*

Gratwick, A. S., *Plautus: Menaechmi* (Cambridge: Cambridge University Press, 1993).

Christenson, David, *Roman Comedy: Five Plays by Plautus and Terence* (Newburyport, MA: Focus Publishing, 2010).

Rouse, W. H. D. (ed.), *The Menaechmi, the Latin Text together with the Elizabethan Translation* (London, 1912.), xiii:

Carlo Goldoni's *I Due Gemelli Veneziani*

Goldoni, C., Bolt, R. (transl.), *The Venetian twins; Mirandolina: two plays* (Bath, England: Absolute Classics, 1993).

William Shakespeare's *The Comedy of Errors*

William Shakespeare, *The Comedy of Errors*, Barbara A. Mowat and Paul Werstine (eds), ser. Folger Shakespeare Library (New York: Washington Square Press: 1996).

François Regnard's *Les Ménechmes ou Les Jumeaux*

Jean-François Regnard, *Les Ménechmes, ou Les Jumeaux, Comédie en Cinq Actes, Précédée d'un Prologue, Théâtre classique*, Ernest et Paul Fièvre (eds) (Publié par Gwénola, Septembre 2015): http://www.theatre-classique.fr/pages/programmes/edition.php?t=../documents/REGNARD_MENECHMES.xml

Richard Rodgers, Lorenz Hart, and George Abbott's *The Boys From Syracuse*

The Boys From Syracuse (Libretto for First Revival (1963) at Theatre Four, New York, Music by Richard Rodgers, Lyrics by Lorenz Hart, Book by George Abbott, based on 'The Comedy of Errors' by William Shakespeare (R&H Theatricals, A Concord Company, 1965)

Notes

Chapter 1

1 For a discussion of the comic fragments and their relationship to Plautus' work, see Wright (1974).

2 Gellius *NA* 3.3.3, 3.3.11; cf. Beare (1964: 45–6).

3 For a concise summary of the manuscript tradition, see Richlin (2005: 4–6); MacCary and Willcock (1976: 233–35); Gratwick (1993: 34–40).

4 Our main sources comprise four writers – Cicero (103 BCE–43 BCE), Pompeius Festus (late 100s CE), Aulus Gellius (fl. 130s CE), and Jerome (fifth century CE) – all of whom lived long after Plautus' own time.

5 Mattingly (1957).

6 See Sedgwick (1949): 379. Erotium's passing remark about Hiero as the 'present king of Syracuse' (411–12) could, theoretically, give us an early *terminus post quem* date of 215, but it is impossible to interpret this line with any certainty.

7 See Moore (1998) and Richlin (2017).

8 Translation Olson (2007: 71–3).

9 Cf. Gnatho in Terence's *Eunuchus*.

10 See especially Nesselrath (1990) and Csapo (2000).

11 The most notable exception, of course, is Plautus' *Amphitruo*, which tells the story of the conception and birth of Hercules. Though it features a divine cast and tells a mythological story, the characters nevertheless fulfil stock domestic roles: Zeus as *adulescens*, Mercury as *callidus servus*, etc.

12 Surviving lines of Menander's *Dis Exapatōn* correspond to lines 494–561 of Plautus' *Bacchides*.

13 For a concise summary of the Plautine innovations to Menander's text, see Marshall (2006: 3) and Barsby (1986: 142–43).

14 Stärk (1989) and Lefèvre (1985: 693–98), argue against a Greek original and consider the play wholly Plautine following the traditions of pre-literary Italian dramatic forms. Those who support the idea of a Greek original include: Lejay (1925: 100), Taladoire (1956: 117), Fantham (1968), Damen (1989), Gratwick (1993), Questa (2004: 72), Maurice (2005), and Lowe (2019), among others.

15 Webster (1970: 71–4) has proposed that *Menaechmi* may have been based on Alexis' *The Brothers*, but the evidence is too fragmentary to confirm this hypothesis.

16 Cf. Arnott (1975: 39–41).

17 See also Hunter (1979: 29, n.34); Damen (1989: 410–12); Gratwick (1993: 23–4, n.6); Primmer (1987) and (1988: 195); Braun (1991: 209, n.6); Masciadri (1996: 98), all cited in Lowe (2019: 215, n.7).

18 Cf. Lowe (2019: 221) who organizes the acts according to the involvement of their protagonists as follows: (1) Menaechmus E, (2), Menaechmus S, (3) Menaechmus S / Menaechmus E, (4) Menaechmus S / Menaechmus E, (5) Menaechmus S + Menaechmus E.

19 See also Damen (1989) and Gratwick (1993: 25–30).

20 For a helpful overview of native Italian pre-literary dramatic forms, see Panayotakis (2005) and (2019).

21 Strabo 5.233 reports that it was continually performed in Oscan dialect throughout its history, pre-dating Plautus and extending through the Augustan era.

22 Marshall (2006: 5–6).

23 Cf. Lowe (2019), especially 217–18, and Stärk (1989).

24 Cf. Marshall (2006: 7–12).

25 Cf. Reynolds (1946), McKeown (1979), Kehoe (1984), and Fantham (1989).

26 Cf. Valerius Maximus 2.10.8, scholion to Juvenal 6.250, Seneca, *Letter* 97.8, Lactantius *Institutes* 1.20, all cited in Marshall (2006: 9).

27 For a very helpful overview of the identity and status of Roman actors, see Richlin (2005: 19–21); Edwards (1997); Beare (1964: 167).

28 See especially Moore (1998), Slater (1985), and Christenson (2019).

29 Moore (2012: 4) helpfully summarizes the sources for music in Roman Comedy as follows: 'descriptions of musical and theatrical performance by ancient authors, extant written music from the ancient world, notation in the late-antique and medieval manuscripts of Plautus and Terence, archaeological and epigraphical evidence for the tibia and for ancient performance, and comparative evidence from other traditions of music and theatre'. See also Moore (2019).

30 Moore (1999: 136–41); on their metres, Wright (1982: 513–14); Boldrini (1992: 91).

31 Cf. Segal (1968).

32 For a general overview of masks, see Duckworth (1952: 88–94); Beare (1964: 186, 309); Wiles (1991: 133–44); and Marshall (2006), especially 126–58.

33 For comprehensive discussions of this rule, see Pickard-Cambridge (1968: 135–6), and Marshall (1994: 94–114).

34 For a helpful chart illustrating how the roles could be divided between three actors, with the same actor playing both twins up until the final recognition scene, see Damen (1989: 412–14). For four actors, see Moorhead (1953: 126).

35 The speaking roles are: Prologue, Peniculus, Menaechmus E, Erotium, Cylindrus, Menaechmus S, Messenio, Erotium's unnamed maid, Menaechmus E's unnamed wife, the old man, and the doctor. The mute characters include: Menaechmus S' porters (*navales pedes*, 350; *istos* 436), the wife's maid 'Deceo' (736), four servants to the old man (990–1009), and possibly additional maids to Erotium (351–56) and to the wife.

36 For comedic costumes in general, see Duckworth (1952: 88–94) and Marshall (2006: 56–66).

37 Cf. the buskin (*cothurnus*) of tragedy.

38 Cf. *Amphitruo* 143–5, in which Mercury calls attention to the little wings on his hat by which the audience can distinguish him from his 'twin', Sosia, and the golden ribbon under Jupiter's hat, by which the audience can tell him apart from Amphitruo.

39 Cf. *Capt.* 778–9.; *Epid.* 194–5, fr. inc. 56, and *Phorm.* 844–5, all cited in Duckworth (1952: 91).

40 For a detailed analysis of the props in *Menaechmi*, see Ketterer (1986: 51–61).

Chapter 2

1 All translations are from Christenson (2010), unless otherwise noted.

2 Cf. Segal (1968) and (2001).

3 Of the twenty-one extant comedies of Plautus, twelve open with a prologue and two delay them beyond the first scene (*Miles Gloriosus* 79–155 and *Cistellaria* 149–202). The other seven plays forgo a prologue altogether.

4 Ten of Plautus' prologues present a plot summary or *argumentum* (*Amphitruo, Aulularia, Captivi, Casina, Cistellaria, Menaechmi, Mercator,*

Miles, Poenulus and *Rudens*); four include prologues without a plot
summary (*Asinaria, Pseudolus, Trinummus* and *Truculentus*); and five omit
a prologue altogether (*Curculio, Epidicus, Mostellaria, Persa* and *Stichus*).
The beginning of *Bacchides* is lost, but the expository dialogue of the early
scenes precludes the need for a prologue. On plays without prologues, and
the exposition of a plot through initial dialogue scenes, see Duckworth
(1952: 212) and Marshall (2006: 194–7). The fragmentary play, *Vidularia*,
seems to have had a prologue, though, as Calderan (1982), Marshall (2006:
195), and Sharrock (2009) surmise, it is unlikely that it provided an
argumentum.

5 Cf. Muecke (1987: 15).

6 Plautus, *Plautini Viginti Comediae*, ed. J. P. Valla and Bernardo Saraceno
   (Venice, 1499) sig. f5v: Menaechmus '*quia meno maneo & aechmi cuspis
   dicitur quod in cuspidine faelicitatis permanserit*' (cited in Hardin [2003-4]:
   263, n. 39).

7 Christenson (2010: 43, n.11) and Gratwick (1982: 104).

8 See Moore (1999: 136–9).

9 For the ubiquity of slaves in Rome in the 200s BCE, and its reflection in the
   performative arts, see McCarthy (2000), Richlin (2014) and (2017).

10 Cf. Klein (2015).

11 McGinn (2003: 21–69).

12 For Roman dowries, see Treggiari (1991: 323–65) and Gardner (1990:
   97–117).

13 Cf. von Staden (1996), Phillips (1980), and Jackson (1993).

14 Alexis fr. 146 (142K). For this fragment and other Greek comic fragments
   featuring doctors, see Arnott (1996: 430–2).

15 Cf. Baumbach (1983).

Chapter 3

1 The popular scene of Xanthius and Dionysius exchanging costumes in
   Aristophanes' *Frogs* (494–673) exemplifies the Mistaken Identity Bit's early
   popularity going back even to Greek Old Comedy.

2 On metatheatre in Plautus, see Barchiesi (1970), Slater (1985; 1990), Moore
   (1998: 67–90), Sharrock (2009), Gowers (1993: 50–108 passim), Muecke

(1986), Hardy (2005), Rosenmeyer (2002), Thumiger (2009) and Batstone (2005), all cited in Christenson's (2019) excellent discussion and digest on the subject.

3   Slater (1985: 154–5): 'The prologue and epilogue in Plautus, then, seem to function not as conventions designed to transmit as briefly as possible the information necessary to understand the play but rather as transitions between nontheatrical and theatrical modes of perception – and of course as opportunities for games-playing in and of themselves. The jokes and banter that seem so irrelevant to a reader actually perform a vital function in alerting the audience to its role in the play and in the workings of the theatre.'

4   Cf. Fontaine (2009) and Karakasis (2019).

5   On female diction in Roman Comedy more broadly, see Adams (1984) and Dutsch (2008).

6   i.e. Erotium at 213, 372, and 424 and the *matrona* at 604, 614, 658 and 752.

7   i.e. Peniculus at 150, 197, 216, 471, 516, 612, 637 and 642; Messenio at 255, 256, 316, 338, 1013, 1029, 1032 and 1066; Menaechmus S at 280, 301, 307, 346, 414, 428, 503, 509, 533, 727, 731, 742, 751, 821, 1060, 1092 and 1093; Menaechmus E at 127, 180, 198, 613, 631, 696 and 1030; Cylindrus at 312 and 329; the *senex* at 821, 872, and 946; the Doctor at 916; and the Lorarii at 1016.

8   See also Zeitlin (1996), Bleisch (1997), Gold (1998) and Richlin (2015) and (2017).

9   See Brown (1995) and (2000) and Traill (2001).

10 For more on improvisation in Roman Comedy, see Marshall (2006: 245–79).

Chapter 4

1   For more a helpful overview of the play's early transmission, see especially Radden Keefe (2019).

2   Tarrant (1983), 302–7. See also Gratwick (1993), 34–40.

3   Gratwick (1993), 35.

4   Candiard (2019), 326

5   Menaechmi (1486), accessed at http://www.apgrd.ox.ac.uk/productions/ production/4500

6 Beacham (1991: 202); Menaechmi (1486), accessed at http://www.apgrd.
   ox.ac.uk/productions/production/4500

7 Uberti (1985), 45.

8 Menaechmi (1486), accessed at http://www.apgrd.ox.ac.uk/productions/
   production/4500

9 Ault (1997), 17–39, offers helpful translations – with commentary – of the
   records of court performances at Ferrara.

10 See Candiard (2019), especially 331–2.

11 See Richards and Richards (1990), especially 11–31.

12 Lea (1962), 173.

13 See Hardin (2003–4), 259–60.

14 By analyzing parallel passages from Ovid and *The Tempest*, Bate (1994), 8,
    lays out persuasive evidence that Shakespeare was a competent Latin
    reader, but relied on an array of sources to do his work (i.e. both
    translations and Latin texts). Cartwright (2016), 75–7, makes a compelling
    case that Shakespeare must have had both Warner and a Latin edition of
    Plautus in front of him as he wrote *The Comedy of Errors*.

15 Dolan (1999), xxxv.

16 See also Miola (1994), especially 20–38.

17 Cf. Gill (1930), 13–65; for a helpful table comparing the two plays scene by
    scene side by side, see especially pp. 26–34.

18 For an analysis of Shakespeare's setting, see Franko (2009), 234–40.

19 All Shakespeare quotes come from Shakespeare (1996).

20 For historical context on the status of servants and slaves in Elizabethan
    England, see Hunt (1997), 39–45.

21 See Pilon (1920), 11–145; Toldo (1903); Gilbert (1859).

22 'Regnard' (1865), 701.

23 All quotations from *Les Ménechmes* come from Regnard (2015). All
    translations are my own.

24 Cf. *Bacchides* Fragment V: '*sicut lacte lactis similest*'

25 On the valet character type in the work of Molière and his successors, see
    Gouvernet (1985).

26 Cf. 4.3.1383-1386, where Ménechme threatens Finette, Araminte's maid.

27 Cf. Segal (1968) and (2001).

28 Goldoni famously employs this gimmick as well in *Servant of Two Masters*
    (1743).

29 See Lancaster (1951), especially 594–7.

30 https://flipbooks.cfregisters.org/R51/index.html#page/442/mode/1up; Cf. Colson (1820), 171.

31 Early records reveal that actresses began performing publicly in Spain and Italy by the end of the sixteenth century, in France by the early seventeenth century, and in England following the restoration of the monarchy in 1660. See Grist (2001), 59, and Lancaster (1951), 596–7.

32 Cf. Chappuzeau (1875), 29: 'I do not know if the sight of men dressed as women, wearing clothes of the opposite sex, which outside of similar occasions and at times of public libations is punishable and forbidden by the laws, is less blameworthy' (*Je ne sçais [sic] s'il est moins blâmable de voir des hommes travestis en femmes & prendre l'habit d'un autre sexe que le leur, ce qui hors de pareilles occasions, & des tems [sic] acordez aux rejouissances publiques, est punissable & defendu par les Loix*).

33 Claretie (1909).

34 All translations come from Bolt (1993). This script was used for the play's British premiere by the Royal Shakespeare Company at the Swan Theatre, Stratford-upon-Avon in 1993. While Ranjit Bolt is identified as the author of the book, Rosanna Bradley is identified as the 'Literal Translator' in the *didascalia* for *The Venetian Twins* (7).

35 https://it.wikisource.org/wiki/I_due_gemelli_veneziani/
L%E2%80%99autore_a_chi_legge

36 Secrest (2001), 201.

37 All page numbers refer to the libretto of first revival of *The Boys From Syracuse* (First Performance April 15, 1963) at Theatre Four, New York, Music by Richard Rodgers, Lyrics by Lorenz Hart, Book by George Abbott, based on 'The Comedy of Errors' by William Shakespeare (R&H Theatricals, A Concord Company, 1965).

38 Secrest (2001), 204.

39 For a beautiful recording of the song from 1938, by the incomparable Miriam Shaw, see: https://archive.org/details/78_sing-for-your-supper_les-brown-and-his-orchestra-miriam-shaw-richard-rodgers-lorenz_
gbia0158816b/SING+FOR+YOUR+SUPPER+-
+Les+Brown+and+his+Orchestra.flac

40 Cf. van Elk (2009).

References

Adams, J. N., 'Female Speech in Latin Comedy', *Antichthon* 18 (1984): 43–77.

Arnott, P. D., *An Introduction to Greek Theatre* (London: Macmillan, 1959).

Arnott, W. G., *Menander, Plautus, Terence* (Oxford: Clarendon Press, 1975).

Arnott, W. G., *Menander: Volume I*, series Loeb Classical Library (Cambridge, MA: Harvard University Press, 1979).

Arnott, W. G., *Alexis The Fragments: A Commentary* (Cambridge: Cambridge University Press, 1996).

Ault, T. 'Classical Humanist Drama Transition: The First Phase of Renaissance Theatre in Ferrara', *Theatre Annual* 50 (1997): 17–39.

Baldwin, T. W., *On the Compositional Genetics of 'The Comedy of Errors'* (Urbana: University of Illinois Press, 1965).

Barchiesi, M., 'Plauto e il "metateatro" antico', *Il Verri* 31 (1970): 113–30.

Barsby, J., *Plautus*, Bacchides (Warminster, Wilts, and Chicago, IL: Aris & Phillips and Bolchazy-Carducci, 1986).

Bate, Jonathan, *Shakespeare and Ovid* (Oxford: Oxford University Press, 1994).

Batstone, W. W., 'Plautine Farce and Plautine Freedom: An Essay on the Value of Metatheatre', in: W. W. Batstone and G. Tissol (eds), *Defining Genre and Gender in Latin Literature* (New York: Peter Lang, 2005), 13–46.

Baumbach, Lydia, 'Quacks then as now? An examination of medical practice, theory and superstition in Plautus' *Menaechmi*', *Acta Classica* XXVI (1983): 99–104.

Beacham, Richard, *The Roman Theater and Its Audience* (London: Routledge, 1991).

Beare, W., *The Roman Stage: A Short History of Latin Drama in the Time of the Republic*. 3rd edition. (London: Methuen, 1964).

Berlanstein, Lenard R., 'Women and Power in Eighteenth-Century France: Actresses at the Comédie-Française', *Feminist Studies*, Vol. 20, No. 3 (1994): 475–506.

Bleisch, Pamela R. 'Plautine Travesties of Gender and Genre: Transvestitism and Tragicomedy in Amphituo', *Didaskalia* 4 (1997): https://www.didaskalia.net/issues/vol4no1/bleisch.html

Boldrini, Sandro, *La prosodia e la metrica dei Romani* (Rome: Carocci, 1992).

Braun, L., 'Keine griechische Originale für Amphitruo und Menaechmi?', *WJA* 17 (1991): 193–215.

Brown, Peter, 'Aeschinus at the Door: Terence, Adelphoe 632-43 and the Traditions of Greco-Roman Comedy', *PLLS* 8 (1995): 71–89.

Brown, Peter, 'Knocking at the Door in fifth-century Greek Tragedy', in: S. Gödde and T. Heinze (eds), *Skenika: Beiträge zum antiken Theater und seiner Rezeption*, Festschrift for H-D. Blume (Darmstadt: Wissenschaftliche Buchgesellschaft, 2000), 1–16.

Calderan, R. (ed.), *Vidularia: Introduzione, testo critic e commento* (Palermo: Vittorietti; Graecolatina, 1982).

Callier, Reina Erin, 'Men In Drag Are Funny: Metatheatricality and Gendered Humor in Aristophanes', *Didaskalia* 10.13 (2014): https://www.didaskalia. net/issues/10/13/

Candiard, C., 'Roman Comedy in Early Modern Italy and France', in: M. Dinter (ed.), *The Cambridge Companion to Roman Comedy*, ser. Cambridge Companions to Literature (Cambridge: Cambridge University Press, 2019), 325–38.

Cardoso, Isabella Tardin 'Comic Technique', in: M. Dinter (ed.), *The Cambridge Companion to Roman Comedy*, ser. Cambridge Companions to Literature (Cambridge: Cambridge University Press, 2019), 120–35.

Chatfield-Taylor, H. C., *Goldoni: A Biography* (New York: Duffield and Company, 1913).

Chappuzeau, Samuel, *Le Theatre François*, Georges Monval (ed.) (Paris: Jules Bonnassies, 1875).

Christenson, David, *Roman Comedy: Five Plays by Plautus and Terence* (Newburyport, MA: Focus Publishing, 2010).

Christenson, David, 'Metatheatre', in: M. Dinter (ed.), *The Cambridge Companion to Roman Comedy*, ser. Cambridge Companions to Literature (Cambridge: Cambridge University Press, 2019), 136–50.

Claretie, Jules, 'Inauguration du monument élevé à la mémoire de Jean-François Regnard, à Dourdans', *Discours*, 5 September (1909): http://www. academie-francaise.fr/inauguration-du-monument-eleve-la-memoire-de-jean-francois-regnard-dourdan

Colson, J. B., *Répertoire du Théâtre Français, ou Détails essentiels sur trois cent soixante tragédies et comédies; ouvrage utile au directeurs et entrepreneurs de spectacle, aux régisseurs, acteurs, à toutes les personnes chargées du service de la scène, et aux amateurs du théâtre* .... (France: Chez l'auteur, 1820), 171–72.

Csapo, Eric. 'From Aristophanes to Menander? Genre transformation in Greek Comedy', in: Mary Depew and Dirk Obbink (eds), *Matrices of Genre:*

Authors, Canons, and Society (Cambridge, MA: Harvard University Press, 2000), 115–33.

Damen, Mark, 'Actors and Act-Divisions in the Greek Original of Plautus' "Menaechmi"', *The Classical World*, Vol. 82, No. 6, (July–August 1989): 409–20.

Damon, Cynthia, *The Mask of the Parasite: A Pathology of Roman Patronage* (Ann Arbor: University of Michigan, 1997).

Davies, Frederick (transl.), *Goldoni: Four Comedies: The Venetian Twins, The Artful Widow, Mirandolina, The Superior Residence* (London: Penguin Books, 1968).

Dinter, Martin T. (ed.), *The Cambridge Companion to Roman Comedy*, ser. Cambridge Companions to Literature (Cambridge: Cambridge University Press, 2019).

Duckworth, George, *The Nature of Roman Comedy* (Princeton: Princeton University Press, 1952).

Dutsch, D. *Feminine Discourse in Roman Comedy: On Echoes and Voices* (Oxford: Oxford University Press, 2008).

Edwards, Catharine, 'Unspeakable Professions: Public Performance and Prostitution in Ancient Rome', in: Judith P. Hallet and Marilyn B. Skinner (eds), *Roman Sexualities* (Princeton, NJ: Princeton University Press, 1997), 66–95.

van Elk, Martine, '"This Sympathizèd One Day's Error": Genre, Representation, and Subjectivity in The Comedy of Errors', *Shakespeare Quarterly*, Vol. 60, No. 1 (2009): 47–72.

Fantham, Elaine, 'Act IV of the Menaechmi: Plautus and His Original', *Classical Philology*, Vol. 63, No. 3 (1968): 175–83.

Fantham, Elaine, 'Mime: The Missing Link in Roman Literary History', *The Classical World*, Vol. 82, No. 3 (1989): 153–63.

Fantham, Elaine, 'Women in Control', in: Dorota Dutsch, Sharon L. James, and David Konstan (eds), *Women in Roman Republican Drama* (Madison: University of Wisconsin Press, 2015), 91–107.

Fontaine, Michael, *Funny Words in Plautine Comedy* (Oxford: Oxford University Press, 2009).

Franko, George Fredric, 'Epidamnus, Thucydides, and "The Comedy of Errors"', *International Journal of the Classical Tradition*, Vol. 16, No. 2, (2009), 234–40.

Gardner, J., *Women in Roman Law and Society* (London: Croom Helm, 1990).

Gilbert, D. -L., 'Regnard: Sa Vie et Ses Oeuvres', *Revue des Deux Mondes*

(1829–1971), 1er Septembre 1859, Second Période, Vol. 23, No. 1 (1859): 167–83.

Gill, Erma M., 'The Plot-Structure of "The Comedy of Errors" in Relation to its Sources', *Studies in English*, No. 10 (1930): 13–65.

Gold, Barbara, 'Vested Interests in Plautus' *Casina*: Cross-Dressing in Roman Comedy', *Helios* 25.1 (1998): 17–29.

Goldberg, Sander M., 'Plautus on the Palatine', *The Journal of Roman Studies* 88 (1998): 1–20.

Goldoni, Carlo, *Memoirs of Carlo Goldoni, written by himself, translated from the original French by John Black; edited, with an introd. by William A. Drake* (New York: Knopf, 1926).

Goldoni, Carlo, *The Comic Theatre*, John W. Miller (transl.) (Lincoln: University of Nebraska Press, 1969), 3.

Goldoni, Carlo, Bolt, R. (transl.), *The Venetian twins; Mirandolina: two plays* (Bath, England: Absolute Classics, 1993).

Gouvernet, G., *Le type du valet chez Molière et ses successeurs, Regnard, Dufresny, Dancourt et Lesage: caractères et évolution* (New York: P. Lang, 1985).

Gowers, E. *The Loaded Table: Representations of Food in Roman Literature* (Oxford: Oxford University Press, 1993).

Gratwick, A. S., 'Drama', in: E. J. Kenney and W. V. Clausen (eds), *The Cambridge History of Classical Literature*, vol. II: *Latin Literature*, 77–137 (Cambridge: Cambridge University Press, 1982).

Gratwick, A. S., *Plautus: Menaechmi* (Cambridge: Cambridge University Press, 1993).

Grist, Elizabeth Rosalind, *The Salon and The Stage: Women and Theatre in Seventeenth-Century France*, Thesis submitted for PhD degree (Queen Mary & Westfield College, University of London, 2001).

Hamilton, Donna B., *Shakespeare and the Politics of Protestant England* (Lexington: University of Kentucky Press, 1992).

Hardin, Richard F., '"Menaechmi" and the Renaissance of Comedy', *Comparative Drama* vol. 37. No. 3/4 (2003–4): 255–74.

Hardy, C. S. 'The Parasite's Daughter: Metatheatrical Costuming in Plautus' Persa', *Classical World* 99 (2005): 25–33.

Henze, Richard, 'The Comedy of Errors: A Freely Binding Chain', *Shakespeare Quarterly*, Vol. 22, No. 1 (1971): 35–41.

Highet, Gilbert, *The Classical Tradition: Greek and Roman Influences on Western Literature* (Oxford: Oxford University Press, 1967).

Hunt, Maurice, 'Slavery, English Servitude, and "The Comedy of Errors"', *English Literary Renaissance*, Vol. 27, No.1 (1997): 31–56.

Hunter, R., 'The comic chorus in the fourth century', *Zeitschrift für Papyrologie und Epigraphik* Bd. 36 (1979): 23–38.

Jackson, R. P. J., 'Roman Medicine: the Practitioners and their Practices', *Aufstieg und Niedergang der romischen welt* II.37.1 (1993): 79–101.

Karakasis, Evangelos, 'The Language of Roman Comedy', in: M. Dinter (ed.), *The Cambridge Companion to Roman Comedy*, ser. Cambridge Companions to Literature (Cambridge: Cambridge University Press, 2019), 151–70.

Kehoe, P. H., 'The Adultery Mime Reconsidered', in: D. F. Bright and E. S. Ramage (eds), *Classical Texts and Their Tradition: Studies in Honor of C. R. Trahnam* (Chico, CA: Scholars Press, 1984), 89–106.

Ketterer, R. C., 'Stage Properties in Plautine Comedy III', *Semiotica* 60 (1986): 29–72.

Klein, V. S., 'When Actions Speak Louder Than Words: Mute Characters in Roman Comedy', *The Classical Journal*, Vol. 111, No. 1, Special Issue on Plautus in Performance (2015): 53–66.

Lancaster, Henry Carrington, *The Comédie Française, 1701-1774: Plays, Actors, Spectators, Finances*, ser. *Transactions of the American Philosophical Society, 1951*, vol. 41, pt. 4 (Philadelphia: American Philosophical Society: 1951).

Lea, K. M., *Italian Popular Comedy: A Study in the Commedia dell'Arte. 1560-1620, 2 vols.* (1934; reprint, New York: Russel and Russell, 1962).

Leach, Eleanor Winsor, 'Meam quom formam noscito: Language and Characterization in the Menaechmi', *Arethusa* 2 (1969): 30–45.

Lefèvre, E., 'Rez. Primmer 1984', *Gnomon* 57 (1985): 693–98.

Legrand, P.-E., *Daos: tableau de la comédie grecque durant la période dite nouvelle* (Lyon and Paris: Rey, 1910).

Lejay, P.-E., *Plaute* (Paris: Boivin, 1925).

Lloyd-Jones, Hugh, 'Menander's Aspis', *Greek, Roman, and Byzantine Studies*, Vol. 12, No. 2 (1971): 175–95.

Lowe, J. C. B., 'Cooks in Plautus', *Classical Antiquity*, Vol. 4, No. 1 (1985): 72–102.

Lowe, Christopher, 'The Structure of Plautus' Menaechmi', *The Classical Quarterly* 69 (2019): 214–21.

Lucas, M. Hippolyte, *Histoire Philosophique et Littéraire du Théatre Français Depuis Son Origine Jusqu'à Nos Jours* (Paris: Librairie de Charles Gosselin, 1843).

MacCary, W. Thomas and Willcock, M. M. (eds), *Plautus* Casina (Cambridge: Cambridge University Press, 1976).

Marshall, C. W., 'The Rule of Three Actors in Practice', *Text and Presentation* 15 (1994): 53–61.

Marshall, C. W., *The Stagecraft and Performance of Roman Comedy* (Cambridge: Cambridge University Press, 2006).

Marshall, C. W., 'Sex Slaves in New Comedy', in: Ben Akrigg and Rob Tordoff (eds), *Slaves and Slavery in Ancient Greek Comic Drama* (Cambridge and New York: Cambridge University Press, 2013), 173–96.

Marshall, C. W., 'Stage Action in Roman Comedy', in: M. Dinter (ed.), *The Cambridge Companion to Roman Comedy*, ser. Cambridge Companions to Literature (Cambridge: Cambridge University Press, 2019), 85–170.

Masciadri, V., *Die antike Verwechslungskomödie, 'Menaechmi', 'Amphitruo' und uhre Verwandtschaft* (Stuttgart: M & P Verlag für Wissenschaft un Forschung, 1996).

Mattingly, H. B., 'The Plautine Didascaliae', *Athenaeum* 35 (1957): 78–88.

Maurice, Lisa, 'A Calculated Comedy of Errors: The Structure of Plautus', *Syllecta Classica* 16 (2005): 31–59.

McKeown, J. C., 'Augustan Elegy and Mime', *Proceedings of the Cambridge Philological Association* 25 (1979): 71–84.

McCarthy, Kathleen, *Slaves, Masters, and the Art of Authority in Plautine Comedy* (Princeton: Princeton University Press, 2000).

McGinn, Thomas A. J., *Prostitution, Sexuality, and the Law in Ancient Rome* (Oxford: Oxford University Press, 2003).

Miola, Robert, *Shakespeare and Classical Comedy: The Influence of Plautus and Terence* (Oxford: Oxford University Press, 1994).

Miola, Robert, 'Roman Comedy in Early Modern England', in: M. Dinter (ed.), *The Cambridge Companion to Roman Comedy*, ser. Cambridge Companions to Literature (Cambridge: Cambridge University Press, 2019), 312–24.

Moore, Timothy J., *The Theater of Plautus: Playing to the Audience* (Austin: University of Texas: 1998).

Moore, Timothy J., 'Facing the Music: Character and Musical Accompaniment in Roman Comedy', *Syllecta Classica*, Vol. 10 (1999): 130–53.

Moore, Timothy J., *Music in Roman Comedy* (Cambridge: Cambridge University Press, 2012)

Moore, Timothy J., 'Music and Metre', in: M. Dinter (ed.), *The Cambridge Companion to Roman Comedy*, ser. Cambridge Companions to Literature (Cambridge: Cambridge University Press, 2019), 101–19.

Moorhead, Paul G. 'The Distribution of Roles in Plautus' *Menaechmi*', *The Classical Journal*, Vol. 49, No. 3 (1953): 123–27.

Muecke, F., 'Plautus and the Theater of Disguise', *Classical Antiquity* 5 (1986): 216–29.

Muecke, F., *Plautus: Menaechmi* (Bristol: Bristol Classical Press, 1987).

Nesselrath, Heinz-Günther, *Die attische mittlere Komödie: ihre Stellung in der antiken Literaturkritik und Literaturgeschichte, Untersuchungen zur antiken Literatur und Geschichte* vol. 36 (Berlin: Walter de Gruyter, 1990).

Nolan, Frederick, *Lorenz Hart: A Poet On Broadway* (Oxford: Oxford University Press, 1995).

Olson, S. Douglas (ed. and transl.), *Athenaeus: The Learned Banqueters, Volume 1: Books 1-3.106e*, ser. Loeb Classical Library (Cambridge, MA: Harvard University Press, 2007).

Panayotakis, Costas, 'Native Italian Drama and Its Influence on Plautus', in: M. Dinter (ed.), *The Cambridge Companion to Roman Comedy*, ser. Cambridge Companions to Literature (Cambridge: Cambridge University Press, 2019), 32–46.

Panayotakis, Costas, 'Comedy, Atellane Farce, and Mime', in: S. J. Harrison (ed.), *A Companion to Latin Literature*, ser. Blackwell Companions to the Ancient World (Malden, MA: Blackwell Publishing, 2005), 130–47.

Pickard-Cambridge, A. W., *The Dramatic Festivals of Athens* (Oxford: Oxford University Press, 1968).

Phillips, Joanne, 'The Emergence of the Greek Medical Profession in the Roman Republic', *Transactions and Proceedings of the College of Physicians of Philadelphia*, series 5, vol. 2 (1980): 267–327.

Pilon, Edmond, 'Preface', in: Jean-François Regnard, *La Provençale*, Collection des Chefs-D'Oeuvre Meconnus (Paris: Éditions Bossard, 1920), 11–145.

Primmer, A., 'Die Handlung der Menaechmi (I)', *WS* 100 (1987): 97–115

Primmer, A., 'Die Handlung der Menaechmi (II)', *WS* 101 (1988): 193–222.

Questa, C. *Sei letture Plautine, Aulularia, Casina, Menaechmi, Miles Gloriosus, Mostellaria, Pseudolus* (Urbino: Quattro Venti, 2004).

Radden Keefe, B., 'The Manuscripts and Illustration of Plautus and Terence', in: M. Dinter (ed.), *The Cambridge Companion to Roman Comedy*, ser. Cambridge Companions to Literature (Cambridge: Cambridge University Press, 2019), 276–96.

Rambo, Eleanor F., 'The Significance of the Wing-Entrances in Roman Comedy', *Classical Philology*, Vol. 10, No. 4, (1915): 411–31.

Regnard, Jean-François, *Théatre de Regnard; Nouvelle Édition, Revue, exactement corrigée, & conforme à la representation*, tome second (A Londres, 1743).

Regnard, Jean-François, *Les Ménechmes, ou Les Jumeaux, Comédie en Cinq Actes, Précédée d'un Prologue, Théâtre classique*, Ernest et Paul Fièvre (eds) (Publié par Gwénola, September 2015): http://www.theatre-classique.fr/pages/programmes/edition.php?t=../documents/REGNARD_MENECHMES.xml

'Regnard', in: *The Atlantic Monthly: A Magazine of Literature, Art and Politics*, Vol, XV, No. LXXXVII (Boston: Ticknor and Fields, 1865), 700–11.

Reynolds, R. W., 'The Adultery Mime', *The Classical Quarterly*, Vol. 40, No. 3/4 (1946): 77–84.

Richards, Kenneth and Richards, Laura, *The Commedia Dell'Arte: A Documentary History* (Oxford: B. Blackwell for Shakespeare Head Press, 1990).

Richlin, Amy, *Rome and the Mysterious Orient: Three Plays By Plautus* (Berkeley: University of California Press, 2005).

Richlin, Amy, 'Talking to Slaves in the Plautine Audience', *Classical Antiquity*, Vol. 33, No, 1 (2014): 174–226.

Richlin, Amy, 'Slave-Woman Drag', in: Dorota Dutsch, Sharon L. James, and David Konstan (eds), *Women in Roman Republican Drama* (Madison: University of Wisconsin Press, 2015), 37–68.

Richlin, Amy, *Slave theater in the Roman Republic: Plautus and popular comedy* (Cambridge and New York: Cambridge University Press, 2017).

Rosenmeyer, T. G. '"Metatheater": An Essay on Overload', *Arion* 10 (2002): 87–119.

Rouse, W. H. D. (ed.), *The Menaechmi, the Latin Text together with the Elizabethan Translation* (London: Catto & Windus, 1912).

Secrest, Meryl, *Somewhere For Me: A Biography of Richard Rodgers* (New York: Knopf, 2001).

Sedgwick, W. B., 'Plautine Chronology', *The American Journal of Philology* 70 (1949): 376–83.

Segal, Erich, *Roman Laughter: The Comedy of Plautus*, ser. Harvard Studies in Comparative Literature (Cambridge, MA: Harvard University Press, 1968).

Segal, Erich, 'The Menaechmi: Roman Comedy of Errors,' in: Erich Segal (ed.), *Oxford Readings in Menander, Plautus, and Terence*, (Oxford and New York: Oxford University Press, 2001), 115–26.

Shakespeare, William, *The Comedy of Errors*, Barbara A. Mowat and Paul Werstine (eds), ser. Folger Shakespeare Library (New York: Washington Square Press: 1996).

Shakespeare, William, *The Comedy of Errors*, Frances E. Dolan (ed.), ser. The Pelican Shakespeare (New York: Penguin Books, 1999).

Shakespeare, William, *The Comedy of Errors*, Kent Cartwright (ed.), The Arden Shakespeare: Third Series (London: Bloomsbury Arden Shakespeare: 2016).

Sharrock, Alison, *Reading Roman Comedy: Poetics and Playfulness in Plautus and Terence* (Cambridge: Cambridge University Press, 2009).

Slater, Niall W., *Plautus in Performance: The Theatre of the Mind* (Princeton NJ: Princeton University Press, 1985).

Slater, Niall W., 'Amphitruo, Bacchae, and Metatheatre', *Lexis* 5–6 (1990): 101–25.

Stärk, E., *Die Menaechmi des Plautus und kein griechisches Original* (ScriptOralia II AI), Reihe A: Altertumswissenschaftliche Reihe, I (Tübingen: Gunter Narr, 1989).

Taladoire, B.-A. *Essai sur le comique de Plaute*, Thèse de Doctorat soutenue devant la Faculté des Lettres de Paris (Monaco, 1956).

Tarrant, R. J., 'Plautus', in: R. J. Reynolds (ed.), *Texts and Transmissions. A Survey of the Latin Classics* (Oxford: Clarendon Press, 1983), 302–7.

Thumiger, C. 'On Ancient and Modern (Meta)theatres: Definitions and Practices', *Materiali e Discussioni* 63 (2009): 9–58.

Toldo, P., 'Études sur le théâtre de Regnard', *Revue d'Histoire littéraire de la France*, 10e Année, No. 1 (1903): 25–62.

Traill, Ariana, 'Knocking on Knemon's Door: Stagecraft and Symbolism in the "Dyskolos"', *Transactions of the American Philological Association*, Vol. 131 (2001): 87–108.

Treggiari, S. M., Iusti Coniuges: *Roman Marriage From Cicero to Apuleius* (Oxford: Oxford University Press, 1991).

Uberti, Maria Luisa (ed.), *Il Menechini di Plauto: Volgarizzamenti rinascimentali* (Ravenna: Longo, 1985).

von Staden, Heinrich, 'Liminal Perils: Early Roman Receptions of Greek Medicine', in: F. J. Ragep and S. Ragep (eds) *Tradition, Transmission, Transformation* (Leiden: Brill, 1996), 369–409.

Webster, T. B. L., *Studies in Later Greek Comedy* (2nd edition) (Manchester: Manchester University Press, 1970), 71–4.

Wiles, D., *The Masks of Menander: Sign and Meaning in Greek and Roman Performance* (Cambridge: Cambridge University Press, 1991).

Wright, John, *Dancing in Chains: The Stylistic Unity of the Comoedia Palliata* (Rome: American Academy, 1974).

Wright, John, 'Plautus', in: T. James Luce (ed.), *Ancient Writers: Greece and Rome*, vol. 1 (New York: Scribner, 1982), 501–23.

Zeitlin, F. I., 'Travesties of Gender and Genre in Aristophanes' *Thesmophoriazusae*', in: *Playing the Other: Gender and Society in Classical Greek Literature* (Chicago: University of Chicago Press, 1996), 375–416.

Online sources

http://www.apgrd.ox.ac.uk/productions/production/4500

http://www.academie-francaise.fr/inauguration-du-monument-eleve-la-memoire-de-jean-francois-regnard-dourdan

https://flipbooks.cfregisters.org/R51/index.html#page/442/mode/1up

http://content.time.com/time/subscriber/article/0,33009,788806,00.html

TWINdex